# Russia's Komfort

## Anthony of Boston

# Table of Contents

*Russia's Komfort*

## Introduction

This book attempts to expose western hypocrisy which often forgets about atrocities carried out by the US military during their illegal occupation of Iraq. With documentation of such crimes on record, human rights organizations and western media have still, nonetheless, continued to single out Russia for war crimes in Ukraine despite having documented in their own reports evidence which shows that Ukrainian forces have also been deploying troops and military equipment into civilian areas, and firing rockets into areas where residential homes are located. This book warns that western hypocrisy and refusal to take an impartial approach will only further polarize the world of geopolitics and prolong the war in Ukraine and also stifle any chance of both Ukraine and Russia coming to peace terms that could end the fighting. Going back to 2014, Ukraine was the first in the conflict to launch missiles on residential areas. This occurred back in July of 2014, before Russia began arming the separatists. The book also explains how the Odessa fire which killed 48 ethnic Russians fostered tensions in eastern Ukraine. This is an attempt to incorporate the Russian perspective into the western one in order to get to the bottom of the conflict with the hopes finding a diplomatic solution. The term "whataboutism" is used to describe those outlooks that question Ukraine's conduct during the conflict. However, when it comes to law, whataboutism is relevant because the application of law is often contingent on the legal paradigm set by the legal approach to other conflicts.

Since the beginning of the Russian invasion of Ukraine, those who have not followed the backdrop of the conflict could only ignorantly sum up the Russian element as "evil." This war began in 2014 and escalated significantly on the heels of one event. That event was the massacre of ethnic Russians in Odessa in 2014, a crime of which no one had been held to account. Prior to the tragedy, unrest broke out throughout Ukraine following then pro-Russian president Viktor Yanukovych's decision not to sign an economic deal with the EU which would have leaned Ukraine closer to the west and further away from its brother nation of Russia. This move on his part was met with protests all throughout Kyiv, which led to his ousting. Heightened tensions would follow between the Ukrainian-speaking populations and Russian-speaking populations in Ukraine, more ominously in the east and south where a majority of pro-Russians banded together in a wave of Russian nationalism. In the city of Odessa, confrontation between pro-Ukrainian and pro-Russian groups erupted on May 2nd of 2014 when pro-Russian groups counter-demonstrated against a pro-Ukrainian march. The pro-Russian demonstrators in Odessa had been accused back in March of 2014 of attempting to separate Odessa from Ukraine, but the pro-Russians in Odessa never made the declaration and only insisted on more autonomy within Odessa, with Odessa becoming "Novorossiya." On May 2nd, in Odessa, clashes between pro-Russian demonstrators and pro-Ukrainian demonstrators occurred in the streets. The beginning of the fighting happened when pro-Russian activists decided to disrupt a Ukrainian unity parade. As violence later ensued, two pro-Ukrainians and four pro-Russians would be killed in the subsequent fighting in which demonstrators from both sides were using petrol bombs, stones and firearms. Reports indicated that the first person to open fire was a pro-Russian activist with an AK-47, which caused the first death during the encounter. Calls were then made on social media for pro-Ukrainian groups to attack the camp that the pro-Russian groups established at Kulikovo Pole in front of the Trade Union House. When the pro-Ukrainians arrived in numbers far greater than that of the pro-Russians, they destroyed the camp, setting it on fire, forcing the pro-Russian activists to take refuge inside the Trade Union Building. Numerous reports circulated that the occupiers of the building set it on fire inadvertently as both sides of the confrontation were throwing Molotov cocktails at each other, but the Kyiv Post reported that pro-Ukrainian groups were throwing the Molotov cocktails into the building through the front entrance, as well as through the windows on the second and fourth floors. Witnesses reported that many who tried to escape the fire were badly beaten by pro-Ukrainian groups. Meanwhile, the police refused to intervene which led to 48 ethnic Russians, some of which were women and children, being killed in the fire. There has been absolutely no accountability by the perpetrators and no justice for the victims of that fire and many residents in Odessa are still harboring resentment even after the Russian invasion of Ukraine in February of 2022. Two months after the Odessa Tragedy, the Ukrainian forces started launching unguided grad rockets into civilian areas in separatist-controlled Donetsk, an act of aggression which killed over a dozen more civilians. Human Rights Watch documented the event, but levied blame on both sides, despite having gathered and documented evidence that there were no separatist fighters or weapons in the residential areas that were struck. The Odessa tragedy in May of 2014, followed by Ukrainian forces' indiscriminate use of unguided grad rockets into civilian areas in July of 2014 prompted Russia to get involved as that same month President Putin of Russia would vow to protect ethnic Russians at home and abroad.

The irony of the war in Ukraine in 2022 is that the Ukrainian president Vlodymyr Zelenskyy was one the verge of addressing the grievances of the ethnic Russians in eastern Ukraine, both on the language front and on the accountability issue regarding the tragedy of Odessa. The country seemed to be on the verge of healing with a leader that is a native Russian speaker. But perhaps it was too late. Zelenskyy's decision to seek Ukraine's admittance into the multi-national bloc called NATO, which is an organization that the international community has allowed to operate with impunity and unaccountability, ultimately triggered a Russian response. This has led to widespread residual effects and fear of nuclear escalation. Unfortunately for Ukraine, the overtures relayed to them by the United States just prior to February 24th, 2022, turned out to be nothing more than empty gestures.

## Chapter 1: International Humanitarian Law

Under International humanitarian law(IHL), all sides of an armed conflict are bound to regulations intended to protect the civilian population. But human rights organizations investigating areas of conflict in Ukraine have failed to approach the matter with a hard-line impartiality integral towards getting both sides of the conflict to evaluate the civilian costs. Instead, groups like Human Rights Watch and Amnesty International, while noting violations on the part of the Ukrainian army in not taking enough precaution when it comes to protecting the civilian population, still chose to single out the occupying Russian force as the sole perpetrator of civilian casualties. The rules of IHL are meant to extract and protect the civilian population from active hostilities, as well as persuade parties in the conflict to keep the civilian population out of the military framework. While not all civilian casualties are considered a war crime, those deaths and severe injuries that occur in civilian populations among civilians usually indicates that either one party in the conflict is perpetrating the atrocities, or both parties are launching strikes from residential neighborhoods, thus evoking return fire, leaving civilians caught in between the shelling. The latter has been the case in Ukraine both since the beginning of the invasion and since 2014 when the Donbas conflict began, and human rights groups are largely aware of this, but continue to downplay how one side of the conflict is also responsible for imperiling residential areas. When it comes to human rights organizations, the importance of impartiality cannot be understated because when the conflict settles down, insurgencies will want to persuade the population to continue fighting. This is the case in Gaza, where militant groups like Hamas and Islamic Jihad's sole purpose is to reclaim all of Israel for the Palestinians. Yet in those cases, at least in years prior to Amnesty International's Apartheid report castigating the state of Israel and recommending that aid which ensures their security be cut off, human rights organizations were very thorough in reporting how both sides of the conflict are endangering and killing civilians. But in the case of Ukraine, the reports lean heavily towards the western sentiment that condemns the Russian invasion of Ukraine and justifies Ukraine's effort to reclaim lost territory regardless of the civilian population. In this sense, human rights investigators have to be careful not to insinuate that the nation under occupation has every justification to do everything in its power to reclaim lost territory no matter how much it endangers the civilian population. Reporting in such a manner could give insurgent groups around the world the impetus to dial up their attacks if they see that Ukrainian forces are allotted a certain pass when it comes to endangering residential areas. Remnant insurgencies in Iraq could also see the report on Ukraine as justification for them to continue trying to reclaim Iraq irrespective of the civilian population.

This book shows how US military tactics in Iraq are near identical to Russia's tactics in Ukraine, which perhaps indicate that the US and Russia follow a similar military protocol. Many of the weapons used in the war in Ukraine are unguided missiles and cluster bombs which are banned in a number of international treaties, but groups like Amnesty International and Human Rights Watch have yet to launch meaningful investigations into Ukraine's use of such weapons in civilian areas, despite documenting them in reports. This negligence on their part could foster an extremely violent Ukrainian insurgency once the Donbas region is either annexed into Russia or completely extracted from Ukraine. Such an insurgency on the part of Ukraine would be no different than those orchestrated by jihadists in Iraq and Gaza. When this becomes the case in regards to Ukraine, the question is, will human rights organizations continue to downplay the civilian toll of Ukrainian efforts to reclaim lost territory despite civilian casualties, but at the same time warn insurgents in Iraq and Gaza about how their actions to reclaim lost territory is endangering the civilian population? This dilemma is why the international community needs to approach the crisis in Ukraine from the vantage point of addressing a global order that cultivates a discombobulated worldview that refuses to adequately keep track of which parties are or aren't in violation of international human rights laws.

All parties in a conflict are subject to the Geneva Conventions and their Additional Protocol, as well as international humanitarian law. Such regulations are applicable to the war in Ukraine, and both sides have to follow the rules that are aimed to protect the civilian population. The rules also require both sides to take every measurable step to conduct their military operations in a way that ensures the safety of the civilian population and ability of non-combatants to escape the fighting. In addition, all sides must distinguish between combatant and non-combatant, and only launch attacks against combatants, which is anyone who has decided to take part in hostilities against an occupying force. Anyone who is not a member of the armed forces, but takes part in facilitating attacks against an occupying force is a combatant and is subject to the Geneva Convention and other protocols and international humanitarian laws meant for protecting the civilian population. Whenever there is doubt, the person in question is suppose to be presumed civilian.

Human Rights Watch and Amnesty International have to remain aware that insurgencies all over the world are carefully watching the situation in Ukraine unfold and are ready to use human rights evaluations of that conflict as a way to show that their goals are no different than that of the Ukrainians—a goal to essentially reclaim lost territory against forces that operate or have operated in a very similar manner to the Russian forces in Ukraine.

Another entity in question is the International Criminal Court (ICC) which has also brought into question its own credibility, seeing that Russia has already been emboldened by ICC reluctance to investigate US war crimes in middle east, a move which can be construed as setting a precedent that justifies preemptive action and invading a nation on the basis of a presumed danger. Not only has Russia taken advantage of this precedent, but other nations can try to follow suit. India can strike Pakistan without warning. Israel can strike Iran. North Korea can strike South Korea. China can strike Taiwan. Turkey could invade Greece. While the US attests that they do not need a separate entity like the ICC to investigate US atrocities in the middle east by pointing to the fact that the US has prosecuted US soldiers who have committed war crimes, the fact that many in those cases were later acquitted or had the charges dropped could lead to Russia doing the same—launching an investigation just to get the ICC off its back, but then later dropping the charges while boasting of having taken the initiative to carry out their own investigation and prosecution. In this manner, US impunity and non-accountability serves as justification for Russia to shun western condemnation of their military operations. And no one in the international community should be surprised, since Human Rights Watch in fact warned about this issue of other nations becoming emboldened by the lack of accountability regarding US impunity in Iraq, Afghanistan, and Syria.

The ICC was initially welcomed as the answer to impunity, and since its inception, 123 nations have joined the court. But to this day, many war crimes committed throughout the world have been left un-investigated and un-prosecuted. Much of the ICC's inquiry into alleged war crimes has been largely symbolic because in many cases the perpetrators are backed by a very robust military force. Most cases in which perpetrators of war crimes—who are high ranking officials—are brought to justice, are usually carried out when regime change or government overthrow has taken place. This was the case with Slobodan Milosevic, former president of Yugoslavia, who was indicted by the International Criminal Tribunal for the former Yugoslavia in 1999(he died during the trial). However, a criminal court recommending regime change could put officials working for the court in very hot water. Moreover, the ICC was created to serve as a mechanism that would step in when nations accused of war crimes would refuse to conduct their own investigation. But as we see was the case with the US, the way for nations to evade this mechanism is by simply obliging to investigate and then later dismiss all charges. It thus becomes a win-win—the ICC is off one's back and the country absolves itself of responsibility. However, this places society under a very dangerous paradigm of justification and can only lead to a cascade of bold military action all over the world. While the reasons for instituting the ICC was backed by legitimate concerns about impunity, since 2002, many feel that the court needs to do better than it has been doing when it comes to holding human rights offenders accountable. But this is unfair due to the fact that the court is only able to demand things that it cannot take by force. There is no enforcement mechanism by which the ICC can use force to enact justice, which is why its very existence is at times effectuating the opposite of its original intention to deter impunity. At the moment, one can argue that the court's refusal and negligence regarding certain perpetrators is very much compelling other nations to balance the scales when they feel the ICC has refused to do so. Much of the ICC's purposes has been carried out against African leaders like the former Congolese rebel leader Bosco Ntaganda, whom they convicted of war crimes and sentenced to 30 years in prison for murder, slavery, and drafting ⌐ildren into the military. The ICC is also investigating the forced deportation of the Rohingya Muslims from Myanmar to India, during which time 24,000 Rohingya Muslims were killed by Myanmar military and Buddhist militia. But as along as nations refuse to recognize the jurisdiction of the ICC, any arrest warrants that the ICC issues against suspected war criminals will ultimately end up being ignored. They currently have 15 arrest warrants issued, but many nations unwilling to help the ICC enforce it, which is why the former president of Sudan, Omar al-Bashir, charged with war crimes, can continue to evade arrest. There is a catch-22 to nations becoming a member of the ICC—they open themselves up to investigation for war crimes. Sooner or later, however, ICC arrest warrants may start being construed as calling for regime change if they are issued for sitting presidents.

The greatest example of impunity has been carried out by NATO forces, both in Libya in 2011 and in Yugoslavia in 1999. The lack of accountability in both conflicts is a major reason why ICC allegations into war crimes in Ukraine will not be taken seriously. NATO has not conducted their own investigations into war crimes committed by their forces, nor has the ICC formally charged the military bloc with any violations despite evidence presented by human rights groups that civilians were killed as a result of NATO strikes. In Libya, in March of 2011, member nations of NATO such as the US, UK, and France conducted an air and ground assault on Mu'ammar al-Gaddafi's forces. The operation was subject to UN Security Council regulation that all sides of the conflict are to do everything possible to prevent civilian casualties. NATO subsequently implemented a no-fly zone over Libya and carried out missions against Libyan military targets over a period of seven months. However, throughout the conflict, civilian areas in Libya were hit by strikes conducted by NATO forces. To this day, NATO has not responded to allegations (other than providing the typical excuse that they never targeted civilians) nor conducted any formal investigation. In 2012, Amnesty International reported that 55 civilians were killed as a result of NATO air strikes in the cities of Tripoli, Zlitan, Majer Sirte, Brega, Surman, and Bani Walid. In addition, one resident told them that a NATO airstrike on September 15th 2011 killed 40 civilians. In many of the other cases of civilian casualties, there was no evidence of military forces or equipment deployed to the site of the airstrike, which implied that the area posed no threat and therefore should not have been attacked. Many of the families interviewed reported seeing no Libyan military maneuvers in the area that would justify their home being struck by rockets. In one attack in Majer, 34 civilians were killed and NATO provided nothing to justify it. In other cases, the victims could not understand why their house was targeted since no one in the house was part of the military or taking part in hostilities. According to ICC policy, since NATO did not take up an investigation over possible war crimes they committed in Libya, then the ICC could step in and launch an investigation. NATO, back in 1999, conducted a number airstrikes in Yugoslavia as part of a military campaign in the Kosovo War. The justification was in response to Yugoslavia's cleansing of ethnic Albanians. The aerial assault carried out by NATO forces lasted close to three months. While Yugoslavia killed over 2000 combatants, as well as nearly 9000 civilians, NATO strikes killed over 500 civilians. Subsequently, Human Rights Watch found no evidence of war crimes and recommended that NATO establish a separate commission to investigate violations of humanitarian law. Human Rights Watch also pointed out the possibility of Yugoslavia using civilians as human shields.

## Chapter 2: The Bucha Massacre

After Russia advanced into Kyiv in early March, capturing Bucha, Hostomel, Vorzel, and Irpin, the Ukrainian forces launched a counteroffensive against a Russian assault that had been stalled by logistical problems, morale issues among Russian soldiers (many of whom where defecting to the Ukrainian side), as well as their own underestimation of heavy artillery manned by Ukrainian soldiers. The west, while largely negligent of Ukraine's need for air support, managed to provide the Ukrainian forces with high-tech weapons, which proved vital during the Ukrainian counter-offensive. Tactical blunders would compel Russian forces to indiscriminately shell Ukrainian cities. Ukraine, however, began to push back against the Russian advance on  March 25th, 2022 and was able to recapture various parts of eastern and western Kyiv. By the end of the month, Russian forces began to retreat, but would leave  mass destruction in their wake, particularly in the town of Bucha, where close  to  1000  civilians  were  found mutilated  and  tortured  by Russian soldiers. By April 1st, the Ukrainian army reclaimed all of Kyiv. Russia, meanwhile, would only  stage  a  second  assault  in other regions of Ukraine, particularly in the east and the south, where Russian forces were already  gaining  ground  against  the Ukrainian resistance. They completely  surrounded  Mariupol  by March 18th before entering the city center on March 24th. Much of the water and food supply had been cut off and those civilians who remained  stuck  there had  to  wait  on  negotiations  for implementing  civilian evacuation corridors,  which  were  often impeded  by Russian shelling  along  evacuation  routes.  Russia  also upscaled  their attacks on Odessa, Mykolaiv, and the Zaporizhzhia Nuclear Power Plant in early April. The Russian forces continued to fight in Kharkiv, shelling Ukrainian positions. Kharkiv is less than  22 miles from the Russian border. When Russian forces mobilized reinforcements to enter the towns of Izium, Sloviansk, and Kramatorsk, Ukraine ordered that Ukrainian-speakers living near eastern Ukraine evacuate towards the western parts of the country. Much of this was owed to a delay in arms shipments to the eastern parts of Ukraine, shipments which had been promised to Ukraine  by  the  west.  Proximity  to  supply  lines  of  arms shipments was also a factor in the delay. At the beginning of the war,  Ukraine's close proximity to supply lines at the Polish border played a critical role in Ukraine being able to resist the initial Russian advance into Kviv, but in the east, Ukrainian forces were further away from those lines, which made it harder to access incoming weapons provided by the west. Thus naturally Russia would have an advantage in the east, considering the fact that Russian forces in that part of the country are in closer proximity to their supply lines of weapons and aid coming from the Russian Federation. Russia was aware of this and subsequently consolidated all of its military personnel in southeastern Ukraine under the single command of Aleksandr Dvomikov.

In Bucha, after the Russian troops fled Kyiv, it had been discovered that war crimes had taken place there. Photo evidence showed scores of dead Ukrainian civilians that had been lined up and shot in the back of the head, execution style. It was reported by Ukrainian newspaper, The Kyiv Independent, that Russian troops killed a number of civilians in Bucha. These victims included people simply transporting food, or families trying to escape the fighting. On March 5th, Russian troops fired upon 2 vehicles, one of which included a mother and her two children.

Bucha Mayor, Anatoliy Fedoruk, reported to various journalists covering the war that war crimes had occurred in Bucha prior to the Russian retreat. He told the Associated Press that during the fighting the volunteers could not even gather the dead for burial because of the endless shelling by Russian forces. Not to mention, dogs were feeding on the human cadavers that laid in the streets. Many in the international community, in solidarity with Mayor Fedoruk, stated emphatically that Russia was guilty of war crimes. The mayor would also compare the massacres in Bucha to the atrocities committed by the Nazis during WWII. Furthermore, evidence of the tragedy came in the form of videos posted on social media, and the mayor had also noted that among the dead in Bucha, were a number of Russian soldiers—hundreds in fact. Ukrainian soldiers reported finding mutilated bodies comprising of men, women, and children in a basement at a summer camp that was used by the Russian forces as a torture chamber. Some of the acts of torture against Ukrainian civilians involved slicing off ears and pulling out teeth. The Ukrainian newspaper, The Kyiv Independent, posted a photo of a man and three naked women under a blanket whom Russian troops attempted to incinerate before retreating from Bucha. It was confirmed by Ukrainian officials that the women were raped and killed, while the men who were murdered in Bucha were killed execution style as many of the dead Ukrainian men were found with their hands tied behind their backs. A large portion of these victims were going about their day—there were many shopping bags alongside the bodies. In one photo, a man was lifeless next to what appeared to be his bike. It was often the case that many of the dead bodies had civilian clothing, making it all the more likely that civilians in Bucha were targeted for execution.

Various news outlets like CNN and BBC aired footage of the scores of dead bodies that lay in the streets, many of which were bounded with legs and arms tied. Some had been shot at point blank range and others were crushed via being run over by tanks. Charred corpses were seen by a playground with evidence of being executed prior to being burned. The style of execution varied from torture to be-headings, to mutilation and incineration. A number of the bodies had been booby trapped. Many of the residents of Bucha described how drunken Russian soldiers were conducting grave acts of terror and sadism against Ukrainian civilians. When forensics arrived in Bucha, they began the process of excavating those dead bodies buried in mass graves--one of those graves was near the St. Andrew the Apostle church. meanwhile, Ukraine was advised to corroborate with the International Criminal Court and gather evidence that would implicate the Russian state of war crimes. Subsequently, it had been discovered that the Russian army was using flechette rounds to maim Ukrainian civilians. Such a mode of offense was considered a violation of humanitarian law. Many residents, who had taken refuge in basements in fear of the Russian presence, confirmed that the dead civilians in Bucha had been murdered by Russian troops. The residents who sought refuge inside their homes were without basic amenities like electricity and had to make use of candles in order to generate heat for boiling water and for cooking meals. They finally appeared in public when Russian troops had evacuated the town, and some first-hand accounts of the massacre cited by news outlets revealed that Russian troops had been taking nearby civilians and using them as basically cannon fodder against the Ukrainian soldiers. One person who was part of a group of Ukrainians executed by Russian soldiers survived by playing dead after being grazed by the executioner's bullet. His group was caught at a checkpoint and taken captive by Russian troops. They were all tortured, but he was the only one to survive the execution. He later arose and sought refuge at a nearby residence.

Many of the Bucha residents describing how the Russian occupation panned out explained to Human Rights Watch that Russian soldiers were going door to door, interrogating residents, and taking from the them, their clothing, jewelry, and other items that they would find useful. The Russian soldiers were also commanding residents to return to their homes, even as resources such as water and food were becoming scarce. The Russia troops continued their assault on the infrastructure of the town. Russian armored vehicles were also firing indiscriminately at buildings, while denying first aid to survivors of the shelling. The residents also explained how Russian troops began digging mass graves for victims of the conflict and for those executed by Russian soldiers. Summary executions were confirmed to have taken place by the Human Rights Watch organization. The New York Times called the massacre at Bucha a "campaign of terror", and noted that Russian soldiers were killing unsuspecting civilians in cold blood, and raping women—some of whom were held captive in a basement and later impregnated as a result of repeated sexual abuse. One resident in Kyiv who witnessed the Bucha occupation by Russian troops and who was present at the headquarters for the Ukrainian defense force when it was raided by Russian military personnel said that the Russians scoured through documents looking for the names of people who participated in the war in Donbas, before targeting them for execution. He then explained how Russian soldiers specifically sought and executed people who were donning tattoos symbolic of far right and Neo-nazi groups, as well as people who had tattoos that were officially associated with Ukraine. He also told journalists that Chechen fighters were killing people indiscriminately. Later, it had come to the attention of the media that Russian soldiers were seizing cell phones of Ukrainian residents and observing content to see if they held anti-Russian views. When this turned out to be the case, Russian soldiers would either arrest the person or execute them.

According to many of the eyewitness accounts, the massacres could be summed up as indiscriminate killings by Russian soldiers against non-combatant Ukrainian civilians, killings that had no justification. One Russian soldier was overheard bragging of his marksmanship, boasting about how he killed 2 Ukrainians inside their apartment by firing through the windows. When it came to rapes, there were roughly 25 girls and women who were raped by Russian soldiers, according to Lyudmyla Denisova, Ukraine's human rights commissioner.

As the Russian state denied the allegations of war crimes and insisted that the massacres were staged by Ukrainian forces, satellite imagery showed—before the Russian retreat from Bucha—what appeared to be humans dead in the same places that the Ukrainian forces reported seeing them after they reclaimed the town in early April. It was confirmed that the killings took place when the Russians occupied Bucha. Both the New York Times and the BBC agreed with the assessment. The images also showed on March 10th what appeared to be mass graves dug out near a church.

Many of the satellite images were verified by drone and video footage that showed Russian troops shooting a civilian walking with a bike. The person turned out to be the same person, shown in another video, laying dead with civilian clothing near a bike. More video evidence gathered showed Russian paratroopers forcing civilians to lay on the ground, while drone footage later showed dead bodies in the exact same spot. These videos were released by the New York Times on May 19th. Mayor Fedoruk confirmed that most of the executions by Russian forces against Ukrainian civilians took place in the Bucha areas of Yablonska, Sklozavodska and Lisova, and that 280 people from Bucha had to be interred in mass graves. The surviving residents of the city were left having to bury 57 other dead Ukrainian civilians, while coroners gathered 100 more dead bodies. Because there was no electricity, the morgue could not accommodate the dead and preserve the bodies via refrigeration, which left the coroners having to pay landscape workers to dig out a mass grave for the victims. The mayor estimated that the number of people killed in the massacre were somewhere in the range of 300, while the deputy mayor, Taras Shapravskyi, estimated that roughly 50 of those 300 were killed execution style. As of April 12, the number killed in the Bucha massacre was said to be around 400. The BBC news later raised the death toll to 500, and then to more than 1000 by May 16th, estimating that 650 of the +1000 were killed directly by Russian soldiers.

The 64th Seperate Motorized Rifle Brigade was identified as the primary occupiers of Bucha during the Russian invasion. They are an infantry brigade connected to the Eastern Military District's 35th Army. Also identified as part of the Russian occupation of Bucha were Chechen Units from the Special Rapid Response Force and the OMON. These military personnel present in Bucha during the massacres were identified by Ukrainian intel. Subsequently, the name of the Russian soldiers were released by Ukrainian media, which was something considered a top priority by those parties seeking to indict the perpetrators of the massacres for war crimes. In addition, German Intel sources were able to intercept radio transmissions of Russian soldiers, and found that the Wagner Group participated in the orchestration of the massacres. It was clear from the evidence that the Russian soldiers considered the operation of mass killings there business as usual or standard modus operandi. Meanwhile, the National Police of Ukraine convened an investigation into the atrocities that occurred in Bucha, and approached the situation much like a typical crime scene. This ran concurrent with requests from the Foreign Ministry of Ukraine to have the International Criminal Court and other international organizations investigate what happened in Bucha and other parts of Kyiv. Russia, on the other hand, sought to initiate a special conference of the UN Security Council to allege that the gruesome aftermath of the Russian withdrawal from Bucha was staged by Ukrainian radicals for the sake of provocation. Russia ordered their own investigation, suspecting Ukraine of pushing false information.

Ukrainian Foreign Minister, Dmytro Kuleba, compared Russia to ISIS, stating that Russia was worse than the Islamic terrorist group. He also proposed that G7 nations implement harsh financial restrictions on Russia. Kyiv Mayor, Vitali Klitschko, called the massacre a genocide of the Ukrainian people with Vladimir Putin directly responsible. President Zelensky arrived in Bucha on April 4th and spoke at the UN Security Council the next day, calling for Russia to be removed from the Council if they refuse to face consequences. He stated that Russia found pleasure in the deliberate killing of civilians, and he also urged the international community to hold Russia accountable for what transpired in Bucha. The atrocities were also condemned by the EU Council. Its president, Charles Michel, promised Ukraine that the EU would do everything in their power to implicate Russia for the crimes committed. NATO and the UN were, as well, appalled upon hearing about what happened in Bucha. Antonio Guterres, Secretary General of the UN, spoke on behalf of the UN, calling for an investigation that would certainly lead to those responsible having to face a war crimes tribunal. The US called for Russia to be suspended from the Human Rights Council, which led to an emergency special session of the UN General Assembly. There, it was voted that Russia be removed from the Council. However, 24 nations voted against the proposal, while 58 abstained. Libya in 2011 was the only other nation to be removed from the Council.

Other European organizations like the European Commission condemned the massacres in Bucha and formally allowed Ukraine to begin an expedited process of joining the European Union(EU). Estonia condemned Russia, and compared the Bucha massacre to the horrors perpetrated by the Nazis and the Soviet Union, and encouraged investigations and criminal proceeding against the orchestraters of the atrocity. The Prime Minister of Slovakia said that what occurred in Bucha was reminiscent of what happened during the Yugoslavia war.

## Chapter 3: Failure to Impartially Investigate

Human Rights Watch (HRW) released a detailed report about what transpired in Bucha during the Russian occupation between March 4th 2022 and March 31st, 2022. However, it was largely one-sided and managed to ignore, despite documentation, that Ukrainian soldiers were hiding weapons in residential homes, a tactic that Hamas uses in Gaza. Still and all, the details recorded by HRW workers who were present in Bucha between April 4th and April 10th made it clear that a plethora of crimes were carried out by Russian troops. These included executing Ukrainian civilians at point blank range, torture, beheadings, and rape, all of which are deemed war crimes according to the Geneva Convention. One of the HRW workers described the situation in Bucha being akin to a crime scene at pretty much every corner. Death permeated throughout the town, and those who inflicted it had no qualms about it, as they effectuated an atrocity that would deeply impact all of humanity. HRW corresponded with 32 residents in Bucha, of whom included the victimized and those watching the terror unfold. Others who provided information to HRW were first responders, coroner teams, physicians, nurses, and municipal workers. HRW also examined all the gathered evidence such as videos and photos taken by the residents in Bucha. However, their investigation could only examine what would constitute only a fragment of the terror carried out by the Russians. The investigation also does not factor in what could have led to the disproportionate aggressive actions on the part of the Russian troops in response to civilians who many have taken part in hostilities. The Ukrainian government advised civilians to take up arms and resist the occupiers, a recommendation that some segments of the media like the Washington Post was concerned about, due to the fact that taking an active part in hostilities automatically gives a person "combatant" status according to the Geneva Convention. Not to mention, it also raises the likelihood of escalation should any civilian-combatant actions trigger a disproportionate response from the occupying forces. This is what happened during the Haditha massacre in Iraq when after taking gunfire from the surrounding areas, US troops marched into residential areas and executed a number of civilians in a war crime of which all the perpetrators would never be punished for.

On April 15, 2022, it was reported that 278 bodies were recovered following the Russian retreat from the area, and many of the 278 bodies were that of non-combatants. Ruslan Kravchenko verified this with HRW. He serves as the chief regional prosecutor in Bucha. Moreover, more bodies were expected to be found—keep in mind that Bucha has a population of 36,000. A funeral home worker confirmed that his team of morticians had no choice but to bury over a dozen bodies near the Church of St. Andrew and All Saints due to the fact that there was no longer anymore room at the morgue to accommodate the growing number of victims in Bucha. Most of those buried near the church were non-combatant civilians. Another person that worked at a funeral home stated that he found and gathered 200 dead bodies in Bucha since the commencement of the invasion on February 24th 2022. These deceased included men, women, and children, but mostly men. The cause of death for nearly all of them was from gunfire, and roughly 50 of the victims showed signs of bondage and torture. Those whose hands were tied, according to the worker, were most likely taken captive and executed. Russian forces were searching specifically for people who participated in the Donbas conflict and who had tattoos symbolizing far right or neo-nazi movements.

During the time HRW was present in Bucha, they recorded 16 confirmed cases of war crimes of which included extrajudicial executions and the deliberate murder of civilians, mostly men. There were a number of people in Bucha that were wounded by gunfire and had suffered wounds in the neck and shoulders. A nine year old girl was shot in the shoulder trying to flee Russian soldiers.

HRW was given information about an execution that occurred in Bucha on March 4th, when the Russians were present. This information was provided by someone who was able to escape Bucha. He relayed that the Russians had taken five men captive and executed one of them by shooting him execution style. HRW was also told about what transpired the next day when a 48 year old man named Viktor Koval was killed as Russian troops raided his home. Meanwhile, the Russian government fiercely denied any reports that Russian troops were killing civilians during the "military operation.", and continued to assert that not a single resident was injured or killed by Russian forces, and that any reports of the contrary was simply orchestrated by Ukrainian authorities. The Russian forces invaded Ukraine on February 24th,2022, but didn't enter Bucha until February 27th, according to the residents of Bucha. Shortly thereafter, the Russian forces were repelled by Ukrainian forces, but were able to gain control of the town on March 5th when they launched a counter offensive the day before. There is no information on where Ukrainian forces were deploying their troops in the beginning phases of the battle at Bucha. Bucha was used by the Russians as a strategic measure for leveraging their assault on Kyiv. During this occupation, Russian troops were ordered to go door to door, detain and execute anyone who helped Ukraine in the Donbas conflict or anyone who was affiliated with far right or Neo-nazi groups. They also searched for weapons. While Both HRW and Amnesty International documented that weapons were found in a civilian house, only Amnesty International confirmed that Ukrainian soldiers hid the weapons in a residential home near Bucha. The Amnesty International report was also more forthright in conveying that Ukrainian forces were prohibited from doing this because it endangered civilians. The HRW report did not mention anything in regards to violations by Ukrainian soldiers nor ask or speculate on how the weapons ended up in the home of two civilians.

During their occupation of Bucha, Russian troops were telling residents that they were there to save them from nazis. The Russian troops also parked their tanks in front of homes in residential areas in order to deter Ukrainian artillery, and refused to tell family members of those detained where they were taking their loved ones. Both of these were serious violations of human rights. Many of the men taken captive were later found dead in various places around Bucha i.e, streets, parks, basements. Not telling family members of the detained where they were taking them constitutes "enforced disappearance" which is considered a war crime by international law. A few of the dead bodies discovered were mined. The Russian troops were using Ukrainian civilians as human shields and made it a point to situate themselves near civilian areas like homes and schools in order to deter Ukrainian artillery bombardments. There is video evidence that confirms this. When it comes to reports of middle east violence, the Russian approach in Bucha is contrary to how this mode of operation is applied in the middle east, specifically as it was the case during the US/NATO invasion of Iraq, Afghanistan, and Libya where the invaded country's insurgents would hide behind the civilian population. In many cases, the only winning strategy that a smaller number of militants can apply against an incoming larger military force is to resort to surprise attacks and ambushes by hiding in places where they would least be expected. Unfortunately, the only way to achieve such is by hiding behind soft targets i.e. schools, hospitals, libraries, and then launching ambush attacks from those positions, which only compromises the safety of civilians in the area. Hamas uses this tactic in Gaza, ISIS/Anti-Assad rebels likely used this in Syria, the Pro-Russian separatists likely applied the tactic during the Donbas conflict. But in the case of the Russian invasion of Ukraine, the invading force is the one primarily applying this strategy of using civilians as human shields. Citing those aforementioned examples, one may extrapolate that in the case of Bucha, Ukrainian forces would be the only ones setting their military equipment near residential homes. However, video footage from social media showed that in Bucha, it was also the Russian forces placing themselves in the midst of residential and civilian areas. But if we observe the war from the vantage point that the conflict began in 2014, both sides making use of the civilian population is of no surprise. Such was rampant during the Donbas conflict.

When Russian forces occupied other residential buildings, they ordered the tenants to relocate to the basement area and leave the front door unlocked, at least according to one case documented by HRW. Residents described how when the Russian troops came upon a door that was locked, they would force their way in and ransack the home. Many of those living in Bucha at the time told HRW that Russian troops shot at people who ventured outside their homes, leaving it likely that residents were placed on a forced lock-down by Russian troops. This is common by military forces. Ukraine imposed a 3 day lock-down on Kyiv residents at the beginning of the war and ordered the military to shoot anyone they see walking the streets. US forces imposed a similar lock-down in Fallujah in 2004. Russia likely applied this in Bucha. Vasyl Yushenko was killed by Russian forces when he stepped out on his balcony for a smoke. One nurse revealed that many injuries occurred among Bucha residents, even among children as she was left having to tend to 10 injured residents, as well as a little girl who was wounded after being shot by Russian soldiers who were trying to stop her from escaping. The man the little girl was with was killed, while she had to have her arm removed.  Residents were also injured in explosions and bombings that occurred near their residence. It was reported that Russian soldiers shelled the town at the beginning of their advance into Bucha "during artillery exchanges" with Ukrainian forces. There is no documentation on what areas Ukrainian soldiers in Bucha were using as a launching pad to fire artillery at Russian targets. It was noted that Russian troops looted various properties, confiscating highly valued items such as jewelry and electronics. Looting for personal use is considered illegal by international laws on warfare. Valuables can only be attained in warfare if some form of compensation is applied.

All entities in war are obligated to abide by international law, as well as the Geneva Convention of 1949 and other additional regulations such as the First Additional Protocol to the Geneva Conventions. Occupational forces are subject to laws of occupation and international human rights law. Random killing, looting, torture, abduction, vicious treatment of detainees are all illegal according to international laws and regulations on warfare and occupation. Violation of these by soldiers who act arbitrarily or by commanders who give such orders to do so constitutes war crimes. Any executive command entities that have knowledge of such acts and refuse to investigate them or punish those responsible are also liable to being charged with war crimes.

Those living in Bucha reported running low on basic necessities like food and water and electricity, and that some people died as a result of this. One person was reliant on an oxygen machine and when the electricity went out, the machine was no longer operable and the person died. Other crimes perpetrated by the Russian forces took place in Adriviika, Hostomel, and Motzyhn, and those working in Bucha expect more casualties to be factored in when evidence in gathered in other areas. Ukrainian police reported 900 Ukrainian citizens dead in Kyiv as a result of the Russian invasion. However, there was no clear assessment on how those victims perished. The chief regional prosecutor, according to HRW, said that there was 600 dead in Bucha alone. These reports by the Ukrainian police and the chief regional prosecutor stood as of April 15, 2022.

The HRW recommended that Ukrainian officials place evidence gathering near the top of their to-do list because such could be imperative for future war crimes prosecution. They also advised that such would require restricting access to areas where mass graved had been dug out, at least until investigators could analyze the bodies and conclude how the victims died, as well as identify them. If the Russians left anything behind, such could also be used to further implicate Russia for war crimes. The HRW also urged other institutional bodies to assist in the investigation to ensure a thorough examination of evidence. If Ukraine decides to become a member of the International Criminal Court(ICC) treaty, they could have their law aligned with the ICC's policies, which would make the war crimes prosecution process easier and more streamlined and help ensure that each victim and their families receive adequate justice. However, nations that recognize the jurisdiction of the court open themselves up to being investigated and prosecuted for war crimes by the ICC. The ICC has also recognized the conflict between Ukraine and Russia as an international war long before 2022, when both nations were being cited for war crimes during the Donbas conflict. Neither Russia nor the US recognizes the court. HRW in their report in Bucha took a different approach from the one they normally apply to their reports of war crimes committed by US troops. HRW normally does not recommend the ICC get involved in war crimes investigations against the US. They normally repeatedly urge US officials to carry out ther own investigation. Conversely, in the Bucha report, HRW does not implore Russian authorities to carry out an investigation of actions carried by their own troops. They instead call for an ICC investigation into Russian war crimes. A clear western bias on the part of HRW explains why Russia shut down the HRW offices in Russia.

Those who were detained by Russian troops during their occupation of Bucha were taken away secretly and executed. There are 9 documented cases of this by the HRW. This has been extrapolated from eyewitness accounts and also by observing how some of the dead were tied up. A number of victims were located on the outskirts of Kyiv around Yablunska street. The number of summary executions could rise as more bodies which show indications of this manner of death continue to be found around Bucha. These type of executions are considered war crimes, regardless of whether or not the victim was a non-combatant, captive, or POW.

A middle aged woman named Iryna described how Russian troops fired upon her home, which was located at the corner of Yablunska street and Vokzalna Streets. This occurred at the beginning of the Russian advance into Bucha on March 5th. The house ended up ablaze, catching fire as a result of the barrage of gunfire. After the residents in the home—the woman, her father, and husband—screamed repeatedly that they were civilians, the Russian soldiers shooting at the house subsequently ordered them to vacate the house and reveal where the nazis were hiding. The Russian soldiers told them, as well as many of the other residents in Bucha, that they were there to save the Bucha residents from nazis. Using documentation, the Russian soldiers had a list of names of people who participated in the Donbas conflict and accused many residents of Bucha of killing pro-Russians during the war in Donbas prior to February 24, 2022. According to Iryna as documented by the HRW, "The soldiers accused us of killing people in Donbas. They accused us of killing the Berkut in Maidan as well. They concluded that we were guilty and should be punished." The Russian soldiers in reference to the Berkut are referring to members of the Berkut anti-riot police force who were killed by protesters during 2014 Maidan protests in Kyiv. After confronting the residents of Iryna's home, the Russians ordered the men who lived there—Oleh who was Iryna's husband and Volodymyr who was Iryna's father—to put out the fire. As Iryna was being interrogated by a Russian soldier, Oleh and Volodymyr were taken to the yard. After being questioned, the Russian soldiers let Volodymyr go, but kept Oleh in their custody before shooting him in the head. His dead body was located outside the yard on the sidewalk, with half his face blown away by the gunshot wound as blood furiously flowed out of his wound onto the sidewalk. According to Iryna, "he was lying with his face down, and blood was pumping out of his left ear. The right side of his face was missing, and brain tissue and blood were coming out of his wound." The soldiers, as Iryna observed, were treating the situation as if it were some form of entertainment. They then informed and threatened to kill Iryna and Volodymyr if they didn't get away from the area. Oleh's body would remain decomposing right there on the sidewalk for the rest of the month until Ukrainian forces and officials arrived and removed it.

On Sadova Street which runs analogous with Yablunska Street, Russian troops took Vasily Nedashkivski and his wife captive on March 17th after finding weapons in their home. Amnesty International's report documented a case near Bucha of which Ukrainian soldiers had taken weapons they took from a Russian armored vehicle and hid them in a residential home. Meanwhile, the two living at the house were taken to another building to be interrogated. Vasily's wife was subsequently released, while Vasily was taken to a place that the Russian forces called "headquarters" and was found dead weeks after. In retrospect, if Ukrainian soldiers did in fact use Vasily's home to hide weapons, it ultimately endangered the residents that lived there and led to Vasily being shot by Russian forces. The Russians never told Vasily's wife, whose name is Tanya, where he was taken. This enforced disappearance aspect applied here constitutes war crimes. Tanya and her neighbor did mention that residents were allowed to leave their homes, but only for water on certain occasions. When the Ukrainian officials found Vasily's body, they also saw the dead body of another man, Igor Lytvynenko. HRW looked into the situation and the staircase that was filled with blood, they saw that Vasily was beaten very badly with cuts on his hands and bruising on his lower stomach. It looked as though he had been nearly bludgeoned to death with repeated blows to the head before being executed. He was later buried in a makeshift grave near his home.

On March 20th, Russian troops shot and killed a man wearing a black track suit. This was overheard by two people living next to the building that the Russian troops who committed the killing were occupying. Prior to the killing, the Russian soldiers told the two to go back inside their apartment and remain there. However, shortly thereafter, they hear commotion between Russian troops and another man before gunfire erupted. The Russians shot and killed the man in a black track suit who yelled "Slava Ukraini" before he was executed. Recovering the body at the time was out of the question since Russian troops occupied and often cooked food in the courtyard where the man's dead body lay. Both the men who overheard the killing had to wait 48 hours before they could recover the body for burial in a makeshift grave. Ukrainian authorities would later retrieved the body from the grave. In social media photos that appeared to show the man as he lay dead in the yard, it showed that his hands were tied with duct tape, but there was no way to confirm if they were tied before he was killed by Russian troops or after.

The basement of a dormitory at the summer camp where Russian troops were conducting torture sessions was located on Vokzalna St. On April 4th, HRW observed five dead bodies there, all of whom were men wearing civilian clothing and whom had been apparently shot. Four of the five had their hands tied behind their backs, while the other sustained gunshot wounds in the chest. Their names were Serhiy Mateshko, Dmytro Shulmeister, Volodymyr Boychenko, Valery Prudko, and Viktor Prudko. The Russians used the camp as a headquarter and spraypainted "V" outside the camp walls. There were designated areas for eating, and not far from the basement was an area dug out for parking armored vehicles. Two other vehicles in the area also had "V" spray-painted on them. "V" was a symbol of support for Russia's invasion of Ukraine. Satellite images showed that armored vehicles were in Bucha near the camp site on February 28th, while the other aforementioned regular vehicles spray-painted with "V" were seen near the site on satellite imagery on March 10th.

In a video recorded by Denys Davydov along Yablunska street on April 1st showed seven dead victims, one of whom had his hands tied behind his back. This video footage was corroborated by another video posted on Facebook on April 2nd that showed those same seven bodies in the exact same spot. This April 2nd video was filmed from a car that drove alongside two other cars, one of which was occupied by three Ukrainian troops. It was presumed that the man who was deceased with his hands tied behind his back was the victim of an execution carried out by the Russian forces. Meanwhile, a funeral home director named Serhii Kaplychnyi reported finding a number of bodies that appeared to have died via execution. These bodies were discovered at various locations in Bucha, such as on Yablubka Street, where he reported seeing eight dead bodies, all of whom suffered gunshot wounds, with six of them having their hands bound together. At the same site but inside the building on Yablunska Street 144, Serhii said he encountered another dead body on the steps going up to the second floor. At first glance, there weren't any visible wounds, but upon further investigation, Serhii discovered a bullet wound in the dead man's heart. A short while later, 20 more bodies were located on Yablunska Street, and 10 of them had their hands tied together, indicating summary executions took place. Serhii noted that the vast majority of victims were killed at near point blank range, some shot in the head. One of the other morticians, Serhii Matiuk said that the number of bodies he gathered from the streets was in the range of 200, and this was from February 28th when the Russians first advanced into Bucha. This funeral home worker said that all of those victims were killed at close range via gunshot to the head or eyes. These victims included men and women, with some dead in the streets, and others in vehicles. However, he reported that he didn't start seeing bodies with their hands tied until a few days after the Russians entered Bucha. But during the time that the Russian were occupying the town, he recorded having seen nearly 50 bodies with their hands bound, indicating that the victims were summarily executed. They also had bruises and gun shots in the legs and hands, which indicated torture.

When it comes to victims that were killed by simply being in the area—seven instances of which were documented by HRW, it is possible that the Russians could have opened fire on them not knowing if they were enemy combatants. Civilians were encouraged by Ukrainian officials to take part in hostilities. However, according to international law, occupying forces are obligated to take take every measure to confirm the status of the target—whether or not they are an enemy combatant or civilian and whether or not they pose an imminent threat. Case and point. On March 5th, on Yablunska Street at the northeast part, two men who were taking refuge in their basement amid artillery bombardments and gunshots decided to have a look outside once the shelling stopped. This was around 4:30pm. They briefly stepped outside to examine the destruction. One of the men who was the son in law of the other man was shot as he was going back inside. He died the next morning as his family repeatedly tried to contact an ambulance or Ukrainian defense forces. The family buried him in a makeshift shallow grave before the local officials would retrieve the body after the Russians left Bucha. Another example of indiscriminate gunfire upon civilians occurred on March 7th. Nikolaii reported to HRW that Russian troops opened fire on him and some of his family members that day while they were outside but inside of their enclosed balcony on the sixth floor of the apartment building they lived at. Nikolaii, his sister and her husband, Vasyl Yushenko were on the balcony where gunfire struck Vasyl in the throat as he was about to light his cigarette. Luckily, he survived. They took him inside and a neighbor was able to apply first aid, saving Vasyl's life. Even as the neighbor was working on Vasyl, another shot was fired into the apartment by the Russian forces. Vasyl ultimately survived as he was evacuated and wheelbarrowed by Nikolaii, his wife and the neighbors to a Kyiv hospital where he recovered and was later discharged. HRW confirmed this report when they visited the apartment on April 6th and saw the bullet impacts on the glass around the balcony, and along the wall and cabinets behind the glass. There were also blood stains on the ground, as well as human tissue. The trajectory and location of the bullet impact from both shots fired at the apartment showed that the Russian forces purposely aimed at the residents.

In another instance of indiscriminate fire, the Russian troops shot and killed Artem, a 37 year old man who went to his garage to retrieve some food items. Just prior, he was sheltering in the basement in an apartment where he and others took refuge, but went to the garage to get food before he was shot. One of the neighbors who lived nearby reported seeing Russian troops near the garage where Artem was sheltering. She then witnessed them open the door there and then open fire before immediately closing the door. His body was later found on March 20th. He was laying dead on his back with a glass jar of dipping sauce cracked open and spilled all over his legs. He was buried nearby in a shallow grave. He had been employed by the Ukrainian military to paint vehicles and during the Russian invasion took refuge in the basement and often supplied food from his own stockpiles to others sheltering with him. This act committed by Russian forces is strikingly similar to how US military killed civilians during the Haditha massacre. Much like the Russians in this case of going to a residence and shooting inside the house without looking to see who was there, US forces in Haditha carried the same manner of operation, shooting into the home without looking to see who was inside. And in Haditha, many inside those homes were women and children, and those US military personnel that killed them, all had their murder charges later dropped. In the case of Bucha, none of the human rights organizations asked if Ukrainian civilians were shooting at Russian troops from their homes. A very important factor considering that civilians were encouraged to take up arms against the Russian forces. When US soldiers carried out their massacre in Haditha, they had first encountered gunfire and suspected that it came from a nearby residential area, prompting them to engage the houses and kill everyone inside. Official US military protocol authorizes US soldiers to destroy any structure, whether civilian or non-civilian, as well those within it if they deem the structure to be a hostile threat. This goes for soldiers on the ground and in the air. Once a structure is perceived to contain enemy combatant activity, US soldiers are within their right, according to military regulation, to decimate the structure and those inside. This is likely similar with most military regulations, including that of Russia's.

On March 12th, a 61 year old man was killed on Yablunska Street. It happened near an apartment building. The victim, llia Navalnyi, had just left his friend's house. The friend said that while he did not see firsthand the killing of llis, he did see Russian troops outside the apartment complex shooting "across the yard" The next morning, llia was found dead 15 meters from the apartment with papers scattered everywhere near his body. The papers were documents related to llia's national ID.

An old man on his walker was shot and killed near a Soviet memorial on the corner of Nove Highway and Vokzalna Streets, according to eyewitnesses Mykola and Serhii B. They relayed to HRW that they encountered the body on March 8th, as it was leaning over dead near the walker with gunshot wounds. HRW investigated the report and went to the area and saw significant damage to the surrounding structures, which indicated that the area was one of high combat activity. There was no way to tell who killed the old man, whether it was directly by Russian troops or by crossfire between Russian troops and Ukrainian resistance.

Just a few days before the discovery of the old man, Russian troops open fired on a man and a young girl. The man Volodymyr Rubalio was killed, but the young girl who was shot in the arm was able to escape and find neighbors who took her to a basement to provide medical treatment. However, the girl's condition worsened and the tissues around her shoulder where she was wounded continued to deteriorate, which led to her arm being amputated after she was finally admitted into a hospital. HRW never documented the girl's name nor was able to confirm the event. However, when they visited the spot where the girl was shot, they did observe blood stains on the ground separated from each other by a few feet, which indicated that two people may have been wounded there. Another man named Oleh who was 33 years old was missing since March 19th and was later found dead under a pile of metal just a few feet from his apartment building. When HRW went to view the area, they noticed blood stains just meters away from the building where a Russian commander was based. The building, following the Russian withdrawal from Bucha, was littered with rations and Russian uniforms. Ultimately, there was no way to determine the circumstances surrounding Oleh's death—whether he was killed there or placed there after having been wounded elsewhere. HRW asserts that because the area was occupied heavily with Russian military personnel, the Russians were aware of Oleh and the circumstances surrounding his death. The wife, however, was not notified about his death; she only found out about it after the Russian withdrawal —this, according to a resident of Bucha who mentioned it to HRW.

Iryna, whose husband was killed back on March 5th, told HRW that after the Russian troops ordered her to leave the yard where they executed her husband, she noticed a woman laying dead near a bicycle just a few feet from the gate. The woman is presumed to be the same woman seen on aerial footage being shot by Russian forces just after she disembarks from her bicycle after turning on Yablunska Street, where numerous Russian military vehicles were stationed. The footage, which was posted on Telegram on April 5th, indicated that the killing took place between late February and March 9th. HRW interviewed both the head person in Ukraine's de-mining unit in Bucha and the head person of the anti-tank brigade also working on de-mining in Bucha. They both reported that a number of dead bodies in Bucha had been booby trapped. The head of the Ukrainian de-mining unit, Lt. Col. Roman Shutylo, discovered on April 8th, two dead bodies that had been booby trapped. Altogether, 20 dead bodies were found to have booby traps and mines on them. Many of these booby traps and mines were devised with hand grenades and anti-personnel mines. The de-miners later shared videos and photos with HRW showing how the traps were constructed and designed to detonate. Anti-personnel mines and booby traps are banned under the 1997 International Mine Ban Treaty, but Russia never signed onto the treaty.

HRW gathered evidence that the Russian forces looted a number of homes during the occupation, taking all sort of valuables like appliances and jewelry. One person in Bucha told HRW that Russian soldiers invaded his neighbor's house after they evacuated Bucha and damaged a number of things there. He also saw many of the goods from the house stockpiled on Russian military vehicles as they departed the area on March 31st. Another person named Tarasevych who lived in Bucha during the Russian occupation, shared photo evidence that Russian troops were taking household items and valuables. The photos revealed Russian military vehicles with a number of items piled onto the roof, items he recognized as belonging to the tenants who had lived in the apartment building that the Russians inhabited. Tarasevych also told HRW that he witnessed Russian soldiers taking goods from an apartment complex and walking out with them. The items were loaded in bags and taken away by Russian soldiers as they left the apartment building on March 31st. According to HRW, there may be the existence of radio intercepts which show that the Russian soldiers discussed acquiring luxury items taken from civilian homes in Bucha and bringing them back to Russia. However, HRW cannot confirm that to be the case with certainty.

HRW verified that the Russian troops used civilian areas as shields against Ukrainian forces and also placed civilians in Bucha on a mandatory lock-down, prohibiting them from leaving their homes. HRW did not inquire about the location of Ukrainian forces at the time—whether or not they were attacking Russian targets from residential areas. But from the report, it was clear that Russian troops parked their military vehicles in front of residential homes, and deployed their forces in residential areas, similar to how the Russia-backed separatists did so during the Donbas war. Therefore, its conclusive that Russian military personnel did not apply every measure possible to avoid the endangerment of civilian areas. It was confirmed on satellite imagery that Russian troops parked two military vehicles right near an apartment complex north of Yablunska Street, with skid marks in areas nearby showing that Russian military vehicles circulated the area regularly. This evidence lines up with that revealed by the photos and videos taken by Tarasevych, which showed Russian forces and artillery situated in civilian areas, including a base for launching mortars which was situated near civilian residences on Sadova Street. Another area occupied by Russian troops and artillery equipment was near schools. HRW documented evidence that Russian troops were using the school as a place to mount artillery and fire upon Ukrainian positions. According to the Safe Schools Declaration, an agreement among 113 countries of which Russian is absent, schools are not to be used for combat or military operations. From April 4th to the 10th, HRW was granted access to see the bodies that were exhumed from a shallow grave near the Church of St. Andrew and All Saints. Five of the dead from that grave appeared to have been killed via execution by Russian soldiers in the basement at the summer camp on Vokzalna Street. All the bodies removed from the mass grave were lined up in a courtyard and wrapped in body-bags that were left open. HRW was able to watch the exhumations on April 8th and 10th. They noted that officials conducting the task were clothed in protective gear and documented via photo and video the bodies taken from the gravesite, as well as all aspects regarding what was on the body. For at least seven days after the Russians left, Bucha remained full of dead bodies, some buried, others laying in the street. Evidence such as blood stains and bullet casing were ubiquitous. All of this evidence would be vital for war crimes litigation against Russia, but the key is gathering the evidence in a timely manner as to not evoke suspicion of tampering or neglect which could lead to evidence being lost, damaged or destroyed. According to HRW, having an efficient storage system and corroboration among multiple international entities is another key that can make a solid case against Russia in regards to war crimes committed in Bucha. As of April, a number of entities have launched probes looking to see if Russia is guilty of war crimes in Bucha and other areas of Ukraine. Many of these investigations will be fused with a confirmation bias that will prevent a thorough assessment. Those entities that intend to investigate include the Ukrainian government, the International Criminal Court(ICC), Germany, and the UN. HRW urges Ukraine to become a member of the ICC so that the Court can have more pedigree as far as conducting a more robust investigation into what occurred in

Bucha, as well developing a "legal framework" outlining how domestic investigation will apply to prosecution at the international level. Ukraine has since 2013 permitted the ICC to assert jurisdiction over war crimes occurring in Ukraine, but Ukraine has yet to officially become a member of the ICC.

In retrospect, HRW had been present in Bucha from April 4th to April 10th, 2022, after the Russians left the town. During this time, the HRW was able to conduct interviews with a number of residents and see the sites where dead bodies were scattered along the street and also those bodies left in the basement of a building located at a children's summer camp. On numerous occasions, HRW was able to travel along Yablunska Street without escort. They observed evidence in the form of photo, video, and satellite imagery, all provided by local officials, residents, and victims of Russian aggression who survived. The interviews were done with a translator on hand. Some of those interviewed chose not to reveal their identity, while others did. The HRW inquiry into what was happening in Bucha started back in early March when the Russians occupied the area, and during such time, HRW conducted most of their correspondence online or in-person with people who managed to get out of Bucha after witnessing what occurred. Throughout their investigation, they seemed to draw conclusions that were motivated both by confirmation bias, as well as evidence gathering. They also applied a methodology in analyzing their findings, that differed from the ones they typically apply after reporting on US war crimes. During their report on Bucha, they made no appeal to Russian authorities to look into allegations of war crimes carried out by their soldiers. They immediately recommended an ICC investigation which is something they normally do not do when it comes to US war crimes. Keep in mind that HRW is a US-based human rights organization.

The Human Rights Watch organization is considered by many entities throughout the world as notoriously bias in how they approach investigating human rights issues. In 2014, an open letter was published excoriating HRW for what many international organizations and scholars all over the world felt was their unfair bias towards the United States and United States foreign policy. The letter was signed by over 100 academics, scholars, as well as some UN officials such as Hans von Sponeck and Richard Falk. Hans von Speck was the former Assistant

Secretary General of the UN, while Richard Falk was the Special Rapporteur on Human Rights in the Palestinian Territories. The letter outlined how members of HRW were former members of US foreign policy agencies. For example, Tom Malinowski was once special adviser to Bill Clinton and later became Assistant Secretary of State for Democracy, Human Rights, and Labor to HRW. Myles Frechette was a former US ambassador to Columbia and eventually became a member of HRW's Americas advisory committee. This was also the case for Michael Shifter, who served as the director for the US government-funded National Endowment for Democracy's Latin America division. However, it must be said that HRW was well aware of how US foreign policy during their war on terror would set a precedent in which other nations will feel justified to act with the same impunity concerning their foreign policy goals. Here is what HRW stated in a 2011 report entitled "Getting Away with Torture The Bush Administration and Mistreatment of Detainees." It concerns US violations of human rights and the residual effects of such:

*The Price of Impunity*
*The US government's disregard for human rights in fighting terrorism in the years following the September 11, 2001 attacks diminished the US' moral standing, set a negative example for other governments, and undermined US government efforts to reduce anti-American militancy around the world.*

*In particular, the CIA's use of torture, enforced disappearance, and secret prisons was illegal, immoral, and counterproductive. These practices tainted the US government's reputation and standing in combating terrorism, negatively affected foreign intelligence cooperation, and sparked anger and resentment among Muslim communities, whose assistance is crucial to uncovering and preventing future global terrorist threats.*

*President Barack Obama took important steps toward setting a new course when he abolished secret CIA prisons and banned the use of torture upon taking office in January 2009. But other measures have yet to be taken, such as ending the practice of indefinite detention without trial, closing the military detention facility at Guantanamo Bay and ending rendition of detainees to countries that practice torture. Most crucially, the US commitment to human rights in combating terrorism will remain suspect unless and until the current administration confronts the past. Only by fully and forthrightly dealing with those responsible for systematic violations of human rights after September 11 will the US government be seen to have surmounted them.*

*Without real accountability for these crimes, those who commit abuses in the name of counterterrorism will point to the US mistreatment of detainees to deflect criticism of their own conduct. Indeed, when a government as dominant and influential as that of the United States openly defies laws prohibiting torture, a bedrock principle of human rights, it virtually invites others to do the same. The US government's much-needed credibility as a proponent of human rights was damaged by the torture revelations and continues to be damaged by the complete impunity for the policymakers implicated in criminal offenses.*

*As in countries that have previously come to grips with torture and other serious crimes by national leaders, there are countervailing political pressures within the United States. Commentators assert that any effort to address past abuses would be politically divisive, and might hinder the Obama administration's ability to achieve pressing policy objectives.*

*This position ignores the high cost of inaction. Any failure to carry out an investigation into torture will be understood globally as purposeful toleration of illegal activity, and as a way to leave the door open to future abuses.[4] The US cannot convincingly claim to have rejected these egregious human rights violations until they are treated as crimes rather than as "policy options."*

*In contrast, the benefits of conducting a credible and impartial criminal investigation are numerous. For example, the US government would send the clearest possible signal that it is committed to repudiating the use of torture. Accountability would boost US moral authority on human rights in counterterrorism in a more concrete and persuasive way than any initiative to date; set a compelling example for governments that the US has criticized for committing human rights abuses and for the populations that suffer from such abuses; and might reveal legal and institutional failings that led to the use of torture, pointing to ways to improve the government's effectiveness in fighting terrorism. It would also sharply reduce the likelihood of foreign investigations and prosecutions of US officials—which have already begun in Spain—based on the principle of universal jurisdiction, since those prosecutions are generally predicated on the responsible government's failure to act.*

With this aspect taken into account, Russia can simply refuse to cooperate with international agencies regarding war crimes in Ukraine and can base this on the fact that since the US is not being held accountable for human rights violations by international agencies or US agencies for that matter, those same international agencies can in no way bring charges upon Russia until they first bring formal charges against the United States. Refusing to do so justifies the consideration that human rights violations are permitted within the international framework. Now in light of that, Russia's policy on Ukraine follows the same justification that the US applied in the middle east. First was the fear that Ukraine would acquire weapons of mass destruction from NATO which is no different than the United States' fear that Saddam Hussein would have acquired from Africa the materials needed to produce weapons of mass destruction. Second justification for Russia's invasion of Ukraine was that Ukraine was actively committing genocide in the Donbas region, killing Russian-speakers, as well as refusing to allow water to flow into Crimea, thereby justifying Russia's decision to invade the country on the grounds of humanitarian aims. United States tried to argue similar for justifying their invasion of Iraq in 2003. So now there is an international legal precedent which tolerates human rights abuses. It becomes the case that immunity from such activities corresponds with a nation's military might—the more military capability, the more immunity essentially. Russia can also rationalize recognizing as autonomous the Donetsk People's Republic and the Luhansk People's Republic due to the Ukrainian government forces shelling civilian areas in their attempt to crack down on the separatists during the Donbas War. This is a similar model applied by the US against Libya and Syria. In Libya in 2011 during the Arab Spring, the US actually went a step further than Russia did on Ukraine. After Gaddaffi, president of Libya at the time, attempted to crackdown on violent separatists in his country while killing civilians in the process, the United States recognized the separatists in Libya as the official ruling authority of the country. The United States did this in Syria as well, recognizing the rebels in Syria as the official ruling authority of the country after Assad attempted to put down separatist elements in his country while killing civilians in the process. Russia, on the other hand, only recognizes the separatists in Ukraine as the official ruling authority within their respective region. Much like the US/NATO intervened in the civil wars occurring in Libya and Syria over what they felt were human rights abuses, Russia is following the same model—intervening in an ongoing civil war taking place in Ukraine where human rights abuses on the part of the Ukrainian military has been recorded and documented by human rights organizations. Double standards, partiality, and confirmation bias is something that will have to be addressed by human rights organizations. Otherwise, various entities around the world will feel justified to act in accordance with how another country was allowed to conduct itself with impunity. The United Nations Human Rights Council set up a commission after the 2021 Gaza War to probe Israel's treatment of Palestinians. The commission is called the Council of Inquiry and they have concluded that Israel's treatment of Palestinians is why Hamas is firing rockets indiscriminately at civilians. But when one considers how the Ukraine war is being covered and investigated, one should not be surprised that Hamas has managed to convince international organizations that their goal is no different than Ukraine's— defending against an occupation. Now going forward, Hamas's actions will not be questioned when escalation resumes in Israel, much like Ukraine's actions during the war with Russia will not be questioned. This is the first time in recent years that Israel has been singled out as catalyst behind the violence in Palestine. The US has condemned the council, and can likely see that ISIS is next in line to become legitimized by international organizations since even they as a terrorist organization can argue that they, much like Hamas and Ukrainian soldiers, are also trying to recapture territory taken from them during an unjust invasion. Human Rights Organizations in recent years have strayed from the more impartial approach and opted to align with political narratives and is now getting into identifying a sole perpetrator, not extracting the civilian population from the military framework, which will further polarize geopolitics around the world. It is clear that the UN and other human rights organization are attempting to make up for mistakes made by them concerning US war crimes, by taking every step to ensure Israel and Russia are held accountable. Still, it creates a standard that does not answer why the US is able to get away with atrocities abroad.

## Chapter 4: Ukraine's War Crimes

After the annexation of Crimea, in which the majority Russian-speaking population there voted in a referendum to join the Russian Federation, Russian-speaking separatists in eastern Ukraine began occupying administrative buildings in the Donetsk and Luhansk areas of the Donbas region, subsequently declaring autonomy from Ukraine. A number of pro-Ukrainian residents in the Donbas region were taken captive by the separatists. While some were eventually released, little information has been released on the exact number executed. In April of 2014, there were two cases of summary execution carried out by the separatists which were confirmed. The bodies of Volodymyr Rybak, a pro-Ukrainian activist, and Yury Popravko, a student who was from Kyiv, were found with signs of torture in the river Torets, near Raigorodok. Still and all, Amnesty International, in investigating claims from both sides, discovered that allegations in many cases were largely exaggerated. However, when this geopolitical affair erupted into armed conflict in June of 2014, escalating significantly in July, the international laws of war became applied to both sides of the conflict.

Between July 12 and July 21st 2014, Human Rights Watch documented war crimes perpetrated by the Ukrainian government forces in the Donbas region. Unlike the Bucha report, HRW in this documentation made it a point to castigate both sides when it came to human rights violations perpetrated by the Ukrainian government forces. This was erroneous because their own evidence showed that separatist fighters or weapons were not in areas in Donetsk that were struck by Ukrainian artillery. HRW reported that unguided grad rockets fired by Ukrainian government forces and Ukrainian militias into residential areas between the timeframe of July 12th 2014 and July 21st 2014 killed 16 civilians and wounded countless others in the Donetsk region. This was a violation of international law which prohibits launching rockets indiscriminately into civilian areas. Keep in mind that this is before Russia began supplying the separatists in Donetsk. Grad rockets are unguided and cannot strike with precision. Despite the report centering around Ukraine's indiscriminate use of grad rockets, HRW did not single out the Ukrainian forces in this report, but also blamed the separatists for deploying fighters and artillery equipment into civilian areas, which according to the report was not the case. Meanwhile, however, Ukrainian forces and government officials denied using grad rockets despite evidence gathered by HRW which made them quite certain that Ukrainian government forces were the ones firing rockets into civilian areas. HRW observed the presence, shape, and angle of impact craters on the ground and on the buildings, and concluded that these were Ukrainian rockets that hit the area. Because of the proximity of the damage to the separatist positions, HRW concluded that the attacks could not have been carried out by the pro-Russian separatists. Some of the rockets hit separatist checkpoints and civilian areas simultaneously. Three civilians in residential areas in Donetsk were killed by rocket strikes carried out by Ukrainian government forces on July 21st. Two days prior to that, four civilians in Donetsk were killed by Ukrainian rockets fired into residential areas. On July 12th, as documented by HRW, six civilians were killed when Ukrainian rockets struck a residential area in Maryinka. HRW identified the type of rockets used in the attacks--"unguided 122-millimeter surface-to-surface Grad artillery rockets launched from multi-barrel rocket launchers with up to 40 launch tubes." These rocket attacks violated international law regarding indiscriminate attacks. Regardless, HRW placed some of the blame on the separatists for not making every effort to avoid deployment of military personnel and equipment into civilian areas. However, the residents they interviewed reported seeing no separatist fighters or military activity in the area. HRW also mentioned in the report that Ukrainian war crimes did not justify separatist maneuvers toward civilian areas during the conflict, noting how the separatists ventured towards the town center after encountering Ukrainian rocket fire which struck their base and residential areas. But the seperatist only moved to the center after evacuating the civilians there. Nonetheless, HRW pointed out in this report that both sides were responsible for the damage caused by Ukrainian rockets being fired into civilian areas. There could have been some confusion on the part HRW in understanding the statements made by Ukrainian officials concerning Donetsk, that caused them to factor both sides as the catalyst for civilian deaths in the area. In one media report, a Ukrainian military spokesman stated that the military operations undertaken in the Donetsk area by Ukrainian forces on July 21st 2014 was a planned offensive against the separatists and that all artillery fired into the area were only targeting separatist fighters. The goal, he asserted, was to repel separatist forces away from the airport. Another media report, this time in a statement from Andriy Lysenko, a member of Ukraine's National Security Council, completely denied that Ukrainian forces had anything to do with the fighting in the Donetsk region during that timeframe of residential areas in Donetsk being bombarded by Ukrainian unguided grad rockets. He claimed that it was the private pro-Kyiv militia groups doing the fighting. In essence, one can extrapolate that he is indicating that private militias were causing civilian casualties in Donetsk. HRW spoke to a number of residents in Donetsk, and many of them said that one rocket struck near the train station around 10:30am. Another rocket, one of the residents said, hit the courtyard area of an apartment building, and killed a woman and injured a man. The woman's name, however, was not verified. When HRW visited the courtyard, they came across a large crater left by the rocket impact and noticed blood right alongside of it. This was right in the middle of the yard. One of the neighbors told HRW that one man was hit by shrapnel from the rocket blast. They also said that none of the separatist fighters, nor their weapons or equipment was in the area, which contradicted earlier reports that separatist fighters were deploying their forces into residential areas and as such were causing residential areas to be hit by rockets aimed for the separatists. Journalists that were present in Donetsk told HRW that another rocket killed two men near a school. This second rocket was only 100 meters from the one that hit the courtyard and killed a woman. Another impact site was discovered in another residential area, but no verification on whether or not civilian casualties resulted. While HRW was present in Donetsk on July 21st, 2014, they themselves were able to hear grad rockets being fired into Donetsk from the northern part of the city. Because of the intensity of the fighting, there was no way to confirm whether or not more civilians in the area were killed.

On July 19, 2014 in the Kuibyshivski district, HRW located five areas in a residential district that was hit by Ukrainian rocket fire on that very day around 4pm. An elderly woman named Valentina Fedorovna who lived on the first floor of the apartment building that was struck by a Ukrainian grad rocket said that she heard a whistling noise turn into a loud bang as she was in her apartment. A short while later a person was knocking on her door asking if anyone was alive. She had been unconscious between the time of the bang and the time someone came and got her out of the five-story building. Another person who lived in the building was hit by shrapnel from the explosion. One piece had gone through her arm, while another punctured her chest. She also heard people in the building screaming in terror. HRW concluded that the rocket had struck the building on the second floor level and traveled through to the first floor where Valentina was at the time. But luckily, the rocket went through the kitchen and bathroom into the basement. She was in the living room at the time, which saved her life. Another rocket hit a courtyard, not far from Valentina's building, and injured four people. One woman had shrapnel from the explosion stuck in her chest. The playground at a school was struck by a grad rocket, and so was a street right in front of a church. HRW reported that a fifth rocket struck a residential home while no one was there.

HRW was certain that the rocket were fired not by private Ukrainian militias, but by the Ukrainian government forces. The trajectory and outcome of large craters in the areas struck by rockets were evidence enough that the rockets were fired by the Ukrainian armed forces. There was also a crater in the school playground which indicted that the rocket had come from a western direction, which further affirmed that it came from the Ukrainian forces since the front-line situated between the separatists and the Ukrainian armed forces, according to the residents in the Kuibyshivski district of Donetsk, were some kilometers west. The separatists confirmed that unguided grad rockets struck their checkpoint and an adjacent area very close to a residential area. HRW investigated the area and confirmed that this was certainly the case. They noticed craters and parts of the grad rocket scattered close to the checkpoint area and the area situated between the residential area and the checkpoint.

On July 12th in the Petrovskyi district in Donetsk, a residential area north of a road that marks off where the frontlines are located was struck by a number of grad rockets fired by the Ukrainian military. Nineteen impact craters were discovered following the attack, and the locals who lived in the residential areas that were struck showed HRW the damage done to their homes. One of the Ukrainian grad rockets struck a home and killed an entire family living on 2 Chugaeya Street. The rocket destroyed the house and garage. Another woman who lived on the same street told HRW that there were no weapons or fighters in the area that justified firing those rockets into the neighborhood. She told HRW: *I was in my room when I first heard a whistling sound. The walls and windows started to shake and then there were many loud bangs. My son was in the kitchen. He came running when the attack started, probably trying to save me, but a shrapnel hit him in the leg. What's here that they wanted to attack? There is no factory here, no fighters, just poor houses.* Her car was destroyed in the attack, while her home suffered severe damage. Her son was wounded by shrapnel. The local police in the area document seven deaths from the rocket fire and showed it to HRW. It was also concluded that the damage and the areas where the craters from the rocket strikes were indicated that the rockets were fired from an area southeast or further south of the southern separatist checkpoint. All the residents stated that there were no separatist fighters or equipment in the area before it was struck by grad rockets. This contradicts the notion that separatist fighters were using residents as human shields. Nonetheless, HRW blamed both sides for endangering civilians despite the evidence provided to them and which they themselves confirmed. And that same day on July 12th at 10pm, another area was struck by a hail of grad rockets. In the village of Maryinka where 10000 residents live, six people were killed during a rocket attack, while 15 were injured. The village was comprised of residential areas, as well as industrial and rural. One person living where the attack occurred said it lasted about 40 seconds. Overall, twelve apartment building were hit directly by rocket fire and HRW observed pieces of grad rockets both around the residential areas and inside of the apartments destroyed during the attack. Prior to it, the separatists were stationed at a checkpoint 800 meters from the outskirts of the village and a number of separatist fighters were deployed to the area between the checkpoint and the residential areas of Maryinka. However, they moved closer to the center after the rocket attack by Ukrainian forces and after the evacuation of residents in the area. Before the attack, no separatist fighters were in residential areas that were struck—this was later confirmed by a journalist who was there at the time. The separatists only came afterwards to evacuate the residents there. The commander of the separatist fighters reported that 22 rockets hit the checkpoint and residential areas. While evidence showed that the rockets came from Ukrainian government forces, a journalist spoke to HRW and told them he spoke to pro-Kiev militia forces stationed in Novomikhaylivka, a village southwest of Maryinka. And they bragged to him about acquiring a grad rocket system that they were using against the separatists. Another person said he observed rockets being fired from the area southwest of Maryinka. The use of grad rockets on civilian areas in eastern Ukraine by Ukrainian forces ultimately provoked Russia into the conflict. Hence why the very next month in August of 2014, Russia announced they were deploying military aid and equipment to the separatist controlled areas in eastern Ukraine.

Later that year on September 23, 2014, it was reported in Russian media that mass graves were found in the Donetsk region in the villages of Komunar and Nyzhnya Krynka. The area had been controlled by the Ukrainian forces' Aidar battalion and the 25th Paratrooper Brigade, up unto 2 days prior on September 21st when the separatists gained control over the villages. The Russian media station covering the situation showed on air 2 graves, with a dead female body in each one. The reporter there was escorted by separatist fighters. The bodies appeared to have suffered torture with each having their hands tied behind their backs. Other media outlets confirmed the report, adding that one of the women killed and buried was pregnant at the time of her death. Aleksandr Zakharchenko, who was serving as the Prime Minister of what the separatists were now calling the Donetsk People's Republic (DPR), told one reporter that there were three grave sites in the area, one with 40 non-combatant civilians. The  two other grave sites consisted of dead soldiers on both the pro-Ukrainian side and pro-Russian separatist side. Shortly thereafter, on the 26th of September, Amnesty International arrived in the area to investigate the claims. They interviewed the locals, as well as DPR officials and fighters stationed there. Amnesty International is headquartered in the UK and is a non-governmental human rights organization. Human Right Watch, on the other hand, is headquartered in the United States in New York. Amnesty International, overall, seem to be more impartial than Human

Rights Watch. In the villages of Komunar and Nyzhnya Krynka, Amnesty International found pertinent evidence that Ukrainian forces carried out at least four extrajudicial executions during the military operation. However, when it came to the total number, Amnesty did not find as many as had been claimed. They found three gave sites consisting of nine dead bodies, four of which were civilians that were summarily executed. One site was located in the village of Nyzhnya Krynka near a military checkpoint with a memorial of flowers and a sign stating "died for Putin's lies" with each of the victim's names and Russian military ID. A DPR fighter told Amnesty International that the men were conducting recon on the area, but went missing, either presumably captured by Ukrainian forces before being executed or killed in combat. It was not clear as to which. The other two grave sites were located near Komunar village at Mine 22. Each grave had two dead bodies that had already been dug up. Pavel Strukov who was the chief investigator over-seeing the investigation reported to Amnesty International that four male bodies were found there. The locals said that both Komunar and Nyzhnya Krynka were controlled by Ukrainian government forces between August 16th and September 22nd of 2014. On September 22nd, separatist forces reclaimed both areas. Amnesty confirmed that the grave sites were made when the Ukrainian government forces and private pro-Kyiv militias were in control of the villages. At least three local residents are believed to have been executed by Ukrainian government forces after last being seen alive on September 11th 2014. One civilian found near the Komunar village near Mine 22 was that of 21 year old Nikita Kolomeytsev who had volunteered for the separatist forces working as a staffer at a check-point, according to his family. He went into hiding when pro-Kyiv forces took over Mine 22 near Komunar village. A few days after he left, Ukrainian forces came to the house of his family and questioned them, looking for information on Nikita and destroying the house in the process. The family reported to Amnesty that the insignia they were wearing were that of the Dnipro-1 battalion. One neighbor, according to Nikita's mother, said that he saw Nikita get arrested, but this person was not interviewed by Amnesty International. Nikita's body was later identified by the mother, and local police concluded he was killed by gunfire. Around the same time of Nikita's disappearance, two other residents went missing. Both lived across the street from each other and grew cannabis inside their homes. One of the victims had been seen visiting checkpoints both when the DPR forces controlled the village and when Ukrainian forces controlled the village. According to his aunt, he disappeared after visiting the outpost when pro-Kyiv forces controlled it. His name was Sergey Tsarenko, a 26-year old man. His friend, Igor Shipilka, age 60, was also a cannabis grower, and went missing after last being seen taken captive by Ukrainian soldiers on September 12th. A third person Vladimir Yashenko, age 55, went missing around the same time as the others and according to residents who lived near his home, his home was occupied by Ukrainian soldiers after he disappeared. Amnesty International could only confirm the extrajudicial execution of Nikita Kolometsev who was found with his hand bound together. Enforced disappearance and extrajudicial execution is a violation of international law.

In looking back, we see how denial among both parties in the conflict affected international investigations. Both human rights organizations, the Human Rights Watch and Amnesty International typically held both parties in the Donbas War liable to the international laws of warfare. When it came to Bucha, however, the Human Rights Watch failed to inquire about the behavior of civilians taking part in hostilities during the time Russia occupied the area—were there actions on the part of civilian-turned-combatants that endangered civilians in the residential areas. Were the Ukrainian fighters firing at Russian troops from residential neighborhoods? The reason this is relevant is because after the unjustified invasion of Iraq by the United States, international human rights organizations held the insurgency in Iraq liable to international laws of warfare, even as they were defending their country from an unjustified invasion. According to the Human Rights Watch "The laws of war do not outlaw insurgent groups or prohibit attacks on legitimate military targets, but they restrict the means and manner of attacks and oblige all forces in a conflict to protect civilians and other non-combatants." The Ukrainian Special Operations Forces were present in Bucha and initially provided resistance against the Russian invasion before being pushed back by the Russian troops. The Russians occupied Bucha throughout March of 2022. Human Rights Watch, however, did not factor in the potential of this operations unit conducting irregular warfare tactics that could have endangered civilians. The Ukrainian Special Operations Forces consists of 2000 personnel, split into 7 regiments among the army and navy. They are trained by the CIA for insurgency warfare and are the main recipients of western military aid. Their presence is very low key and as of yet, there has been no confirmation on Ukrainian SOF casualties during the Russian invasion of Ukraine.

Following the Russian invasion of Ukraine, male civilians looking to flee the country were ordered to stay or face mandatory conscription into the Ukrainian military. On March 3rd 2022, a week after Ukraine declared Martial law throughout the country in response to the Russian invasion of Ukraine, a decree was made by the Ukrainian government that civilians who get weapons have the legal right to fire upon Russian soldiers and will have the same rights as Ukrainian soldiers. This decree under the Geneva convention essentially made anyone in Ukraine who had a weapon a "combatant." The decree also made it legal for those armed Ukrainian civilians to kill Russian soldiers in Ukraine. In doing so, any armed civilians in Ukraine became subject to international laws meant to protect civilians during armed conflict. Those Ukrainians who chose not to take up arms but stay in Ukraine were entitled to protections that both sides of the conflict had to honor. In the case of Bucha, as defined under the Geneva Convention on who is legally a combatant, those who took up arms upon the approach of the Russian military convoy into Bucha fell under the definition of combatant under Geneva Convention:

*Convention (III) relative to the Treatment of Prisoners of War. Geneva, 12 August 1949.*

*Article 4 A (6)*
*(6) Inhabitants of a non-occupied territory, who on the approach of the enemy spontaneously take up arms to resist the invading forces, without having had time to form themselves into regular armed units, provided they carry arms openly and respect the laws and customs of war.*

Those who fell under this this definition were required by international law to disembark from civilian areas, as those

Ukrainian civilians who did not participate in hostilities against the Russian forces were protected by International Humanitarian Law. This law was applicable during the Donbas War and is the case following the Russian invasion of Ukraine. While it was confirmed that Russia violated those protections during their occupation of Bucha, killing a number of innocent civilians disproportionately to any resistance they may have faced from Ukrainian civilians, the Human Rights Watch, unlike their approach of blaming both sides for the initial firing of grad rockets upon civilian areas by Ukrainian forces in 2014 before Russia got involved in the conflict.,  failed to mention the role that combatants firing upon Russian soldiers in residential areas had on endangering other non-combatant Ukrainian civilians in the area. Both sides of the conflict were subject to take every precaution to protect the civilian population:

*Protocol Additional to the Geneva Conventions of 12 August 1949, and relating to the Protection of Victims of International Armed Conflicts (Protocol I), 8 June 1977.*
*PRECAUTIONS AGAINST THE EFFECTS OF ATTACKS*

*Article 58 -- Precautions against the effects of attacks*

*The Parties to the conflict shall, to the maximum extent feasible:*

*(a) without prejudice to Article 49 [ Link ] of the Fourth Convention, endeavour to remove the civilian population, individual civilians and civilian objects under their control from the vicinity of military objectives;*

*(b) avoid locating military objectives within or near densely populated areas;*

*(c) take the other necessary precautions to protect the civilian population, individual civilians and civilian objects under their control against the dangers resulting from military operations.*

We can observe how back in July of 2014 when it was clear to HRW that the separatists took every precaution to avoid civilian areas (*residents confirmed there were no weapons or fighters in the area)* as Ukrainian forces fired grad rockets into civilian areas, they still nonetheless even after documenting such evidence, implicated both sides as not doing enough to protect the civilian population. In Bucha, HRW didn't question what impact Ukrainian "combatants" had on the situation or what steps combatants on the Ukrainian side were required by international law to take in minimizing damage to civilian areas and civilians. Amnesty International on the other hand did note in their report on Bucha and other nearby villages  concerning the possibility of Ukrainian soldiers endangering civilians in the area. This part of Amnesty International's report called "HE'S NOT COMING BACK: WAR CRIMES IN NORTHWEST AREAS OF KYIV OBLAST" documented the killing of a 15 year old boy, Igor Denchik, and his aunt, Ludmila Shabanova, by Russian soldiers right outside of their basement where the rest of the family was taking refuge. The Russian soldiers had banged on the door and thrown tear gas into the basement before ordering everyone rushing out the basement to get on the ground. That was when the 15 year old boy and his aunt were shot dead. There around 40-50 people in the basement, according to the boy's grandfather. Afterwards it was reported that weapons were found in the house. Here is the excerpt from Amnesty International's report:

*"Timoshenko and another building resident said that in the days following the killing of Igor Denchik and Ludmila Shabanova they learned that the soldiers had searched the basement of the house and found some weapons and/or ammunition which Ukrainian forces or volunteers had recovered from a Russian armoured vehicle which had been struck and immobilized by Ukrainian forces in the area. If in fact Ukrainian forces or volunteers had hidden weapons in a residential building full of civilians, such action would have endangered the safety of the civilians, contrary to their obligation to take all feasible precautions to protect civilians under their control from the effects of attacks, including by avoiding locating military objectives within densely populated areas."*

Amnesty International also stated in that same report, but regarding the town of Borodyanka, that there was evidence that Ukrainian soldiers were using residential buildings to fire upon

Russian military. On March 1st and 2nd, the Russians conducted a series of airstrikes upon residential buildings where 600 families lived. Most of the occupants of the building had gone to find shelter in the basement and many killed as a result of airstrikes were killed in the basement area. 40 civilians were killed when the damage caused many of the buildings to collapse. While it was clear that the attack was disproportionate to the threat, Amnesty International nonetheless pointed out the potential evidence that Ukrainian soldiers endangered civilians by using the apartment as a base to fire upon Russian military:

*There is some evidence that at least at certain moments Ukrainian forces or their armed supporters were using the buildings as a platform from which to fire upon Russian military vehicles transiting the area. A resident of one of the buildings, who spoke on the phone and sent text messages to a relative before his building was hit, said that Ukrainian snipers were on the rooftop and behind the building shooting at Russian convoys; he was afraid that this would lead to Russian retaliation. If it is true that Ukrainian forces were firing from the buildings, they were irresponsibly putting civilians in danger and violating the laws of war. Nonetheless, given the substantial number of civilians that would be expected to be found in these buildings, such large-scale Russian attacks were both disproportionate and indiscriminate under international humanitarian law, and as such constitute war crimes.*

While Human Rights Watch and Amnesty International are both western based, Amnesty International has shown itself far more impartial than Human Rights Watch on its coverage and inquiry into events pertaining to the Ukraine/Russia conflict. This is why Russia should re-open Amnesty International's Moscow office, but completely avoid Human Rights Watch, an organization that has been engulfed by the contrarian and divergent political framework in the United States. What is meant by that is that Human Rights Watch is more concerned about how an international affair confirms the politically charged narrative in the US, as opposed to how the international affair, for example the Russia/Ukraine war, is built upon those events which led up to the conflict and are directly related to the two nations involved in it. The United

Nations has also been affected by the US political framework in their inquiry into the Israel/Palestine conflict following the 2021 Gaza War. Ultimately, it could be perilous for the international community to allow the schismatic political framework in the US to poison the sober outlook of geopolitical events that is required for maintaining a stable and integrated global community. While Amnesty is affected by that as well, they still seem to be able to retain some sobriety on global geopolitical issues, and this is why it is imperative for Russia to reinstate Amnesty's offices in Russia.

## Chapter 5: Reactions to the Bucha Massacre

A number of EU countries have expelled Russian diplomats from their countries, and so did Japan. Both China and India's representatives on the United Nations Security Council referred to the atrocities in Bucha carried out by Russian forces as deeply disturbing. China, however, as a nation that has been conciliatory towards Russia throughout the conflict, resisted pointing the finger directly at Russia. They even broadcast Russia's statements disputing the claims made by Ukraine on what transpired in Bucha. Belarus's president went a step further and denied the claims altogether and accused British operatives in Ukraine of conducting a false flag attack in Bucha to make it seem like the Russians were responsible just so Britain could levy more sanctions on Russia. He also claimed to have evidence in the form of documentation confirming this to be the case, and that he has already presented the documents to the Kremlin. The US, as well as Britain, called for Russia to be indicted on charges of committing war crimes. They also expressed that more sanctions should be applied to the Russian state, while more weapons be sent to Ukraine. But many believe that the supply of weapons into Ukraine will only prolong the war and cause more civilian casualties, a prospect that is even more likely due to the fact that the west will not supply Ukraine with the weapons that would at least allow Ukraine to end the war on their own terms. France, meanwhile, has also accused Russia of violating the laws of war and agreed that sanctions were justified and should be applied towards Russian energy industries of coal and oil. Following French President Macron's statement, the EU placed a ban prohibiting the EU from importing Russian coal, wood, fertilizer, cement, and rubber. This turned out to be a huge expense for Russia that would amount to 8 billion euros annually.

Following reports of what occurred in Bucha, the Russians denied that they ordered the killing of civilians. The Foreign Minister of Russia agreed with the assessment of the Belarusian president that it was a hoax or false flag attack that was staged. According to the Russian Foreign Minister, because reports of dead civilians were not presented until four days after the Russians left, the Ukrainian soldiers must have staged it all. However, the Associated Press confirmed that the mayor of Bucha was reporting dead civilians there back in early March. In another instance where it was confirmed by satellite imagery that Ukrainian civilians were being killed during the time the Russians occupied the town, the Russian representative to the UN insisted that the bodies shown after the Russians left Bucha were not there during the time of their occupation. The Russian Defense Minstry went on to state on Telegram that Russian troops were not targeting civilians during their operation in Bucha, which is the common answer used by most nations accused of war crimes. Ukraine during the Donbas War, the United States, Israel and even Hamas has used that defense. Moreover, the Russian Defense Ministry stated that those killed in Bucha were killed by Ukrainian airstrikes and that the bodies shown in the videos could be seen moving. The BBC later ruled out that the videos were choreographed. One of the most highly regarded sources of the BBC, a media firm called Bellingcat, pointed out how Russian media and a member of Bucha's city council Taras Shapravsky stated that the Russians left Bucha on April 1st at the latest. In Russia, it was clear that there were attempts to paint the Bucha narrative as staged. In one instance, a video was aired on Russian state TV and purported to show that Ukrainians were using mannequins to set up the Bucha hoax. However, this was debunked when it was confirmed that the video was the filming taking place on a television set in Saint Petersburg, Russia. This was confirmed by those who were on set at that time. Another video showed Ukrainian soldiers using cables to pull dead bodies, and was purported in that case to be their staging of the Bucha massacre. But Associated Press stated that cables were used as a precaution due to the fact that some of the bodies in Bucha had been booby trapped. This was confirmed by investigators.

In the online community, the expressing of hatred for east Slavic people was condoned on a number of media platforms. On the pro-Russian side, there were numerous comments on the media app Telegram by Russian nationalists condoning the massacre in Bucha and calling for more attacks on Ukrainians. Some went as far as advocating the extermination of the race altogether. All of this was according to an analysis of pro-Russian channels on the Telegram app. The study noted a strong religious element to much of the hate being expressed. There was homophobia and one of the Russian activists-journalist from

Odessa, the city where 48 pro-Russian activists were trapped and burned alive at the Trade Union Building in 2014, referred to Ukrainians trapped the Mariupol as cockroaches and who should be murdered. On the other side, Facebook and Instagram, American social networking services, had began allowing users in some countries to post messages calling for the murder of Russian nationals and the Russian president. This was according to internal emails that were leaked, which showed that Meta, formerly Facebook, was going to alter its hate speech rules for the Ukraine/Russia war to allow users in countries in close proximity to the war to call for the death of both the Russian president and Belarusian president. This was a u-turn on Facebook's policy regarding incitement of violence. As long as the post was in regards to the invasion of Ukraine, users on Facebook were allowed to call for the death of Russian people and Russian soldiers.

## Chapter 6: The Russian Advance on Mariupol

After the Bucha massacre and Russian pull-out of Kyiv, the Russian military began a second offensive in the southeast of Ukraine. It was announced on April 8th 2022 that the troops there would be consolidated under the command of General Aleksandr Dvomikov, who was given control over the military there, including the military personnel that had originally been deployed to the north and northeastern front before withdrawing from those areas and being relocated to the southeast. Around mid-April, the Russian advance was stifled by resistance in Mariupol where Ukrainian troops had taken positions in abandoned steel factories and remained defiant to Russia's calls for surrender. This assault of Mariupol at this time was a second invasion that started in Kharkiv and stretched to Donetsk and Luhansk. Even though the Russians pulled out of Kyiv, they still fired missiles to the north and west, striking some parts of Kyiv and Lyiv. The Russian troops launched a rocket attack on a Kramatorsk railway station in the Donbas region which killed 52 people and injured up to 300 people. After confirming that the Russian forces had withdrawn from the north and western parts of Ukraine, the US announced that a renewed Russian offensive in the southeast was underway. The evidence from satellite imagery on April 11th showed Russian military units relocating from the northeast to the southeast of Ukraine. Much of the slowed progress was not only due to the Ukrainian resistance at the steel factory in Mariupol, but also due to Ukrainian troops cutting off access between Kharkiv and Izium by demolishing a bridge that connected the two. Nonetheless, the Russians in a matter of days completely surrounded Mariupol and expanded further in other parts of the Donbas region in Donetsk, Luhansk and Kharkiv. Ukraine, in response, sought to undertake a defensive maneuver that would coincide with their retreat as the Russians advanced into Kharkiv and Izium. After the Russian advance was repelled in Kharkiv by Ukrainian troops who managed to destroy critical infrastructure, keeping the Russian forces at bay, the Russian troops subsequently moved their forces to the Donetsk and Luhansk areas. Severodonetsk, located in Luhansk and under Ukrainian control at the time, was bombarded by Russian artillery and seized by Russian forces on May 23rd. The Russians also continued to fire rockets upon Mykolaiv and Odessa and vowed to continue pushing westward after Mariupol would be captured by the Russian forces. This was contrary to Russia's claim that their intentions in Ukraine had changed from hunting nazis to gaining control of the Donbas region. The Russians at this time were intent on capturing Transnistria so that they could block Ukraine's access to the Black Sea. This announcement was followed by explosions in Transnistria on April 27th. Two broadcast towers there which were used for airing Russian TV were decimated. Meanwhile, Russia continued their assault on Odessa, firing rockets at runways, mainly for the sake of cutting Ukrainian supply logistics.

In mid-April 2022 at the steel factory called Azovstal Iron and Steel Works located in Mariupol, Ukrainian defense forces took refuge there and conducted a final resistance to Russian forces. Many believed that because of the number of civilians taking refuge there as well, Ukrainian soldiers were intending to use them as human shields as they fought back against Russian artillery. When Russian troops made their way further into Mariupol and surrounded the factory, Ukrainian forces remained adamant to fight till the last man. However, roughly 1000 Ukrainian remained trapped in the factory. Back in February at the start of the invasion of Ukraine, Russia launched an amphibious assault on Mariupol and shelled it relentlessly, killing 10 Greek civilians and a 6 year old girl. Back in 2015, Russian artillery strikes killed 29 civilians in Mariupol. By the end of February/early March of 2022, Mariupol, though still under Ukrainian control, was completely surrounded by Russian forces whose shelling of the city cut off access to water, internet, and electricity. A teenager was killed as a result of Russian shelling and water was cut off on March 2nd as the Russians were preventing  civilians from evacuating the city. That same day, according to the deputy mayor of Mariupol, hundreds of civilians were killed after  a residential area  was shelled relentlessly by Russian forces. The next day, the shelling continued as the DPR urged Ukrainian fighters to surrender or face guided artillery strikes. The Russian Ministry of Defense reported that the Russian troops seized more areas nearby. Meanwhile, the supplies in Mariupol were gradually running low, and calls were made for reinforcements as  well as the evacuation of civilians just as the Russian forces continued to shell critical lifelines such as hospitals. Finally, a ceasefire was subsequently enacted so that the 200,000 civilians trapped in Mariupol could evacuate. The Red Cross got involved as a facilitator and promised to ensure the establishment of ceasefire agreements which would enable civilians to exit the city. When the ceasefire was finally in place, civilians were only briefly allowed to vacate Mariupol and seek refuge in the city of Zaporizhzhia. Reason being, is because the Russian forces commenced shelling the city which forced civilians to turn back and stay put. Russia's understanding of the ceasefire was that civilians would be allowed to leave, but through a corridor towards Russia, not towards Zaporizhzhia. Ukraine, however, feared that Russia would send Ukrainian civilians held captive to secret concentration camps either in Russia or separatist held areas. This first attempt on March 5th at establishing humanitarian corridors only resulted in 17 people evacuating. The second try the next day was once again subverted by Russian artillery strikes which destroyed the city's fuel pipeline and access to heat in much of the city. 700,000 people were now without heat and in danger of freezing to death in temperatures that had gone below zero. The last remaining communication line, a cellular tower, was damaged by Russian shelling. The Red Cross said that the new ceasefire was in principle only and that much of the other circumstances surrounding how civilians would evacuate remained vague. One of the roads that was going to be used to evacuate civilians was mined. And on March 8th, Russian forces shelled one of the evacuation routes as civilians were being evacuated. Large numbers of civilians were killed in Mariupol and many were buried in mass graves. Even as this was taking place, Russia managed to shell the gravesites where many victims were being buried. An attempt at another ceasefire was stifled on March 9th, when Russian forces began shooting at construction workers and checkpoints established for evacuation. This was followed by an airstrike on a maternity ward and hospital where three civilians were killed and 17 wounded. Three days later, as Russian troops captured the eastern parts of Mariupol, roughly 82 ethnic Greeks were able to get out of Mariupol through one of the corridors established. This was followed by more artillery bombardments of Mariupol by Russian forces. Vadym Boychenko, the mayor of Mariupol, said that on March 13th, the Russian military unleashed hundreds of bombs in a 24 hour period as food and water had become extremely scarce. The Ukrainian forces were, nonetheless, able to provide some resistance and destroy a number of Russian military vehicles as well as kill 150 Russian troops fighting in the city. Meanwhile, ethnic Turks were on standby waiting to be rescued and evacuated by the Turkish government. On March 14th, a convoy of evacuees were allowed to evacuate Mariupol, and the Russian Defense Ministry confirmed that aid was being supplied to the city. The next day on March 15th, even more civilians were able to leave, roughly 20,000. On March 16th, however, a theater in Mariupol where hundreds of civilians had taken refuge was hit by a Russian airstrike. It was reported that 600 people were killed as a result. The assault continued when 2 days later the DPR forces seized the Mariupol airport, driving out the Ukrainian forces. When the DPR advanced, shortly thereafter, into the center of Mariupol, clashes between them and the Ukrainian forces took place at the Azovstal Steel plant. During this time, allegations that Russia was deporting civilians to camps and remote areas of Russia began circulating. After Russia denied that such allegation were true, another school was bombed in Mariupol, a school that was being used by 400 civilians to shelter themselves from the shelling taking place in the city. In the meantime, the Russian forces continued to demand that Ukraine surrender. However Ukrainian forces continued to refuse. On March 21st, Russia responded with a barrage of airstrikes which led the mayor and other city officials to flee shortly after. The Russians at this point were going around the center of Mariupol declaring victory as Russian troops advanced deeper into the city. On March 27th, the mayor called for an immediate evacuation of the remaining residents in Mariupol because food and water had been totally depleted to the point that even Ukrainian soldiers had nothing to consume. Despite such deprivation, Ukrainian soldiers insisted on fighting to the last man, leaving neither civilian nor soldier behind. The next day, the mayor admitted that Mariupol was under Russian control and that 5000 people had perished during the siege. Ukraine reported that 20000-30000 had been captured by Russian forces and sent to camps located in Russia. That same day on March 28th, the Russians occupied the military headquarters, administrative building, as well as the headquarters of the Azov regiment. The Russians, throughout the conflict, were also stopping the flow of aid, shooting down 90% of the rescue helicopters sent by Ukrainian President Zelenskyy to conduct evacuations as well as resupply the

Azov soldiers taking cover at the Azovstal Steel plant. The Ukrainian military had no choice but to eventually splinter into multiple cells after the Russians captured 267 marines from the 503rd Battalion of the Ukrainian Naval Forces on April 4th. This caused a rift among Ukrainian fighters from the Azov regiment and the 36th Separate Marine Brigade, whose lines of communication had been broken by the surrender of the 267 marines of the 503rd Battalion of Ukraine's Naval forces. Ukraine, in response, attempted to resupply the Azov fighters stationed in the Azovstal steel factory, but the deliveries could not be made due to Russian fighters shooting down the MI-8s used for the mission. After the Russians captured the bridge leading to the Azovstal steel factory, they were able to take control of the fishing port and cut the line of access between the Ukrainian soldiers at the fishing port and those at the steel factory. This was a major blow that coincided with a severe shortage of ammo that limited the amount of resistance that the Ukrainian troops holding out at the factory could apply against incoming Russian soldiers. At this juncture, it was easy to forecast that Mariupol would, within a short time, fall into the hands of the DPR and Russian forces. A number of Ukrainian troops from the pocket of Ukrainian soldiers from the 36th Separate Marine Brigade held up at the Ilich steel plant were taken captive on April 11th. Some of them managed to escape and join with the Azov regiment at the Azovstal steel plant, while others were killed en route. The leader, Baranyuk, was captured by Russian forces as he tried to flee the city rather than link up with the Azov. The remaining 1,026 Ukrainian fighters at the Ilich steel plant surrendered the next day, which left Mariupol to be defended by two small pockets of Ukrainian soldiers. Unsurprisingly, the Azov leadership was disappointed with Baranyuk because he did not relay the plan to escape the Ilich steel plant with other military personnel, nor try to link up with the Azov regiment as others who escaped the plant would try to do. Instead, he, as Ilia Samoilenko would express, tried to flee "taking with him people, tanks and ammunition." Subsequently, Ukrainian fighters surrounded by Russian forces at the Azovstal plant requested reinforcement and more supplies, informing the Ukrainian command that the situation was dire, but that fighting was still possible.. The steel plant was a strong fortification and there were many underground tunnels that allowed people there to take cover and remain safe from air strikes by Russian forces. It also provided stealth to Ukrainian troops which made it even harder for enemy forces to locate them. However, without a supply line, there was no way for Ukrainian forces to fend off continuous Russian strikes because ammunition, food, and water would eventually run out and leave those sheltered there with no choice but to either surrender or die from destitution.

After a port was captured near Mariupol's beach, some of the Azov fighters from the Azovstal plant rescued and evacuated the 500 Ukrainian troops and police surrounded at the port. According to an officer of the Ukrainian Marines, the Azov breached the port and provided cover fire for the Ukrainian troops stuck at the port, allowing them to escape. This left those Azov regiment and other Ukrainian fighters at the Azovstal steel plant as the last remaining pocket of Ukrainian soldiers resisting the Russian advance. Yet, they refused to surrender amid Russia's threats to annihilate them. The remaining number of Ukrainian fighters were estimated to be around 2900, according to Russian officials. Even in light of the Russian control over the city, the Russian troops had not yet been ordered to raid the Azovstal plant. It was believed by the Kremlin that Ukrainian forces would surrender once they ran out of critical supplies. But Ukrainian officials took it to mean that Russia was admitting that they had no ability to infiltrate the complex infrastructure of the plant. The subterranean aspects of the steel plant is akin to the methods used by ISIS and Hamas to successfully evade airstrikes in the middle east. However, Russia's main goal in Mariupol was connecting the city to Crimea so that water and other supplies could flow there. Once this goal was reached, Russia felt no rush to take control of the steel plant, figuring that an all-out assault there would needlessly waste military personnel and be extremely costly.

On April 22nd, Russian troops began expanding their presence outside the Azovstal steel plant very close to the positions of Ukrainian soldiers in Azovstal. It was confirmed that day that the only remaining Ukrainian forces in Mariupol were those hiding out in the steel plant. Subsequently, Russia began pulling some of its troops out of Mariupol and reassigning them to other parts of eastern Ukraine. This was followed by a barrage of airstrikes on the Azovstal facility by Russian forces, one of them striking a military field hospital, wounding hundreds more. Just after this on April 30th, a humanitarian corridor was established which was brokered by Antonio Guterres when he visited Moscow the week before. Gradually at the start of May, civilians hiding in the Azovstal facility were being allowed to leave. 100 left Mariupol on May 2$^{nd}$, while Russia pulled many of its forces out of the city and redeployed them elsewhere in the Donbas region. This was confirmed by the US Department of Defense. Folowing the pull-out, Russia's offensive in Mariupol had become strictly airstrikes. The following day on May 3$^{rd}$, however, the Russians attempted to breach the plant through the tunnel system after they had been tipped off on the location of the underground network by an electrician in what was an act of treachery on his part. Two days later, more civilians had been evacuated from the Azovstal facility through a humanitarian corridor designated to operate between 8am and 6pm.

The Russians in a final ploy to get Ukrainian troops at the Azovstal facility to surrender, used thermobaric bombs on Ukrainian soldiers. After a long standoff by the Azov regiment and other Ukrainian fighters, President Zelenskyy would give the order for Ukrainian forces in Mariupol to surrender. This comes after he vowed not to cede any territory to Russian forces. Subsequently, the remaining civilians would be completely evacuated by May 7$^{th}$. The remaining soldiers who came out to negotiate surrender were taken captive by Russian soldiers who would evacuate them from the plant, treat those who were wounded, and detain them along with the remaining Ukrainian soldiers at an area controlled by the DPR forces. The Ukrainian command confirmed that the battle was over and Mariupol was now in the hands of the DPR and Russian forces. The last remaining Ukrainian soldiers surrendered to the Russians on May 20$^{th}$. The Russian president Vladimir Putin promised to treat the prisoners of war according to international standards. However, some in the Russian government were against allowing members of the Azov regiment to be released in the case of future prisoner swaps.

Later, Russian troops discovered over a hundred dead Ukrainian soldiers in a refrigerated truck with explosive booby traps set underneath them. Russia subsequently returned the bodies to the Ukrainian authorities who continue to negotiate with the Russians for a prisoner swap deal.

The situation in Mariupol throughout the conflict was very dire. Throughout March, residents there were left having to scrape up whatever food and water they could find. One of the advisers to the mayor reported that some of the residents of Mariupol had reached a point where they had to drink from puddles to survive. The intense shelling that occurred in the city cut off access to clean water, as well as electricity and communications. The Russian forces were also repeatedly bombing areas that were relegated for the evacuation of civilians, which forced residents to stay put and further endure the depravity and lack of food and water. It was reported that 350,000 residents in Mariupol had little to no access to basic necessities and because of the shelling were afraid to leave their homes to acquire items needed for survival. On March 22nd, eleven buses carrying supplies of basic items to be delivered to those stranded in Mariupol were seized by Russian forces, according to CNN, who also reported that the items on the buses were later confiscated. In addition, the workers who were on the buses trying to transport the supplies to the residents were detained. Ukraine would excoriate Russian forces for restricting residents from acquiring basic items. They also accused Russian General Mikhail Mizintsev of ordering the airstrikes on the children's hospital, maternity ward, and the Mariupol theater. The strikes on the maternity ward and children's hospital resulted in 3 deaths. While the number killed in the theater strike was contested and varied among sources. Russia denied the accusations that they were targeting civilians, and stated that the buildings were occupied by the Azov regiment. The Russian Embassy referred to the video showing a pregnant woman being carried out on a stretcher after the bombing as being staged with the pregnant woman being an actress. But yet it was confirmed that the pregnant woman later died from her injuries on March 13th after the unborn child passed away. Russia, nonetheless, continued to maintain that the hospital was being used as a military post. Three days later, the city theater, where hundreds of residents had taken refuge, was destroyed by a Russian airstrike. However, there were conflicting reports on how many were inside at the time of the strike. Human Rights Watch said that there were 500 civilians inside. Serhiy Taruta, a former governor of Donetsk, on the other hand, said there were over 1000. On satellite footage, there appeared to be the Russian word for "children" impressed on the ground both in the front and back of the theater, put there to indicate that there were children inside. Russia maintained that it was the Azov regiment that bombed the building, not Russia's air force. After the attack, over 100 of the people inside hiding in the basement survived and emerged from the theater debris on March 17th. Ukrainian officials initially reported that there was no one killed during the strike, but later estimated that 300 had been killed. The Associated Press, however, said that 600 were killed as a result of the Russian airstrike. Both of these estimates are based on speculation on the number of people present in the theater prior to the attack. The Associated Press went as far as saying that those killed during the strike were pulverized. The Russians eventually removed the debris and bodies from the theater disaster, but provided no details on the number of civilians who died during the attack. Afterwards, Petro Andriushchenko, an adviser to the mayor of Mariupol, said on social media "Now we will never know how many civilians from Mariupol were actually killed by a Russian bomb at the Drama Theater. The victims were buried under unnamed numbers in a mass grave in Mangush," One survivor of the theater blast, a man named Dmytro Velychko, who was inside at the time of the attack, gave an interview to The Economist and reported that while there were over 1000 people sheltered in the theater, many of them had already moved out days before the bombing, and that on the day of the airstrike, no more than 300 people were inside. He also stated that the current estimates of the death toll from the theater bombing was very exaggerated. He stated that the number of people who died in the attack was in the range of 100, which is a far cry from the 600 that the Associated Press reported.

The deputy mayor of Mariupol reported that one of the residential neighborhoods in Mariupol was shelled relentlessly in a targeted attack that lasted 15 hours. Other evidence such as satellite imagery emerged showing significant destruction to residential infrastructure around Mariupol. Officials estimated that 80% of the residential homes had been destroyed in endless shelling of the city. Images taken by drones showed near apocalyptic scenes of smoke, debris and ashes spread out all over the city. Many in the west insisted that the Russians were targeting residential areas, as well as hospitals and schools. It was reported that 90% of the hospitals in Mariupol were destroyed as a result of

Russian artillery. The overall death toll of civilians, according to Mariupol officials was somewhere in the range of 20000.

Another factor that could implicate Russian for war crimes is the alleged use of chemical weapons. The Azov regiment reported that Russian forces were using a toxin that causes respiratory distress. However, these allegation were never confirmed, but Britain and Ukraine suspected that Russia could have used white phosphorus which is not designated to be a chemical weapon under international regulations.

The Associated Press maintained extensive coverage on the ground in Mariupol, having two journalists working on the scene between late February and early March. At this time, they were just two among only a few international media workers in Mariupol during the Russian invasion. Much of the Associated Press's coverage was used by western media to depict what was taking place there throughout the conflict. Later, on March 11th, they were safely evacuated from the Mariupol by Ukrainian troops.

Between March 16th and March 21st, Amnesty International was present in Mariupol and conducted an investigation as to who was responsible for the attack on the Donetsk Regional Academic Drama Theater. They gathered evidence and did several interviews with survivors and witnesses of the bombing. Amnesty concluded that the number of fatalities were much lower than what has been reported by Ukrainian officials and the Associated Press. The exaggeration on the part of Ukraine and western media, however, did not nullify the fact that the attack was indeed carried out by Russian forces, which Amnesty International confirmed. The Amnesty report did mention that the  number of civilians present at the theater decreased dramatically between March 14th and March 15th, which confirms the testimony of theater bombing survivor, Dmytro Velychko, in his interview with The Economist. Altogether, according to Amnesty's report which is entitled, "CHILDREN" THE ATTACK ON THE DONETSK REGIONAL ACADEMIC DRAMA THEATRE IN MARIUPOL, UKRAINE, roughly a dozen or so people died in the attack, with any remaining possible victims unlikely to be verified. This estimate is even lower than Dmytro's, who estimated the number of victims to be around 100, which is still far less than that given by Ukrainian officials and the Associated Press.

## Chapter 7: Actions of Ukrainian Soldiers in Mariupol

While western backed human rights organizations ignored what maneuvers Ukrainian forces may have used in Mariupol, maneuvers which could have endangered civilian areas, it was reported by an Italian journalist named Vittorio Rangeloni, who has been in the Donbas region since 2015, that following the Russian invasion of Ukraine on February 24, 2022, members of the Azov regiment were using residential neighborhoods in Mariupol to fire upon Russian military, before setting the homes on fire upon leaving. In his report, he interviewed a number of residents in Mariupol after the hospital and theater attack and documented their revelations that members of the Azov regiment started taking defensive positions in residential areas, as well as in schools and hospitals after the Russians bombed Azov military bases soon after arriving in Mariupol in late February. According to the Italian journalist's report, because their military instillation was destroyed, Ukrainian and Azov soldiers began abandoning their trenches and started deploying into residential areas as self-preservation began to take over. As the report would state, this made it easier for Ukrainian soldiers but imperiled the civilians. This video was filmed on April 15th, 2022 and uploaded to Youtube on April 30th. Here is the testimony of some of the Mariupol residents.

One women in Mariupol who was interviewed stated: *We lived for 10 days in the basement. I live here, on the 9th floor. The apartment is still there......I'd like to say I still live here, half the building being destroyed. I hope they help us to rebuild. From here you can see how it was hit. They were cornered so they[Ukrainian army] went it, they entered the building..... They came in and started to open all the doors, from the 4th to the 8th floor on this side, said they had to control the streets.*

Another woman in Mariupol was interviewed by Rangeloni;
*I live here, in Stroitely Street. .......We were kicked out by the Azov soldiers so we went back to the house that was burned on Metallurgov street until the guys from Donetsk helped us, giving us food, drink, and calming us. We didn't even know what was going on. They had forced us to escape. They[Azov regiment]*

*launched Molotovs, according to their plans.......Before leaving, they set fire to our house. The building was all destroyed. Only a few apartments remained. That's where we are now. .....They[Azov] went around like zombies. We asked them why did they shoot, told them not to do it, but they said it was the Russians shooting. And yet we saw with our own eyes how they set fire to the house. They gave us 15 minutes to pack our things, saying there would be planes bombing later. This was in the morning. There were no planes. They burned down the house and they left towards the sea coast.*

This is an interview with a man who gave Rangeloni a tour of a damaged apartment building:

*Here there were many ammunition boxes.....This is also their stuff (he points to weapons the ground near a window along the staircase). They broke all locks and shot from the windows of the apartments. They broke into all the apartments. This is a MON (anti-personnel mine). ....They [Azov] sent everyone away...This is what they used to open the doors(pointing to a piece of metal on the ground) ...Here is a machine gun, and there the barrel(he points at the gun near the window along the stairwell). They were on the fourth floor, teared down the walls joining all the apartments. When they[Azov] left, they burned everything.*

A woman in Mariupol was interviewed: *It's sad, when we ourselves are Ukrainian citizens. This Army that doesn't defend us, should at least not harm us. When you get home and they tell you to go away because they must build barricades and live there, it's horrible. We are Ukrainian citizens like them, they have their obligations, but we are victims of the events. Back there you can see the Azovstal. Here the first bombs fell. ....(The interviewer then asks from what direction did they come)...*

She replies: *From there [From the direction of the Azovstal factory]. ......from the very beginning. Even when there were still no Russians in this area. We had the impression they wanted to destroy it on purpose. They targeted the houses, you saw them, all without roof. My impression is that it was on purpose, so that it didn't belong to anyone. Yes, despite that many people lived here, now they're left without anything, everything it took them a lifetime to build.*

Here is an interview with a group of people interviewed—3 women and a male.
(the interviewers asks them where do you live now)
*In the basement..........8 people in the basement. 11 in the stairs. We share a basement. ........There were 4 days of bombing. It started when Ukrainians entered the building. They left on the forth day. They dropped something from the top floors. A 16 year old boy had his foot cut. The soldiers said to piss on it and he would recover. There were 120 people in the basements. ......The Ukrainians fired[from the houses]. They occupied two floors. First they said they would only coordinate, but then they started also to fire from here. It started from that, and then continued. When we got out, we were shocked. We found RPGs on many floors. Here there were many children. We tried to cook here over a fire under the whistling of the bombs. We got out to ask them to move away, but we were ignored. They didn't want to see us. They said they were following their orders. They said "we are defending our land" But we don't know what they defended. They had no interest in the 120 people living here with cold, hunger. This is how it happened*

-This was from the transcript of the video which was posted online on April 28, 2022 by user
V-N Rangeloni. Here is the url of his video
https://www.youtube.com/watch?v=9Ec6d-JRStw
This is his video with the English translation
https://www.youtube.com/watch?v=y55wF4lo47o
uploaded online by user Tom.

While such evidence should evoke western suspicion, neither HRW nor Amnesty International has yet to launch an inquiry in Mariupol concerning where Ukrainian forces were deploying during the time of the siege.

The one-sided narrative put forth by the west has cultivated a great deal of mistrust, and has compelled many in the west to rely on alternate sources of information in order to develop a broader scope on exactly what is happening throughout the conflict. This mistrust has shown itself never more apparent when on June 27th 2022, Russian forces fired rockets into central Kremenchuk, Poltava Oblast, striking a shopping mall and a nearby factory. The name of the factory was the Kredmash road machinery plant, and was believed to be a military target housing western weapons. The Russians fired 2 Kh-22 anti-ship missiles from the Shaykovka air base in the Kaluga region. The first missile reportedly hit the far end of the Amstor mall, causing the shopping center to become engulfed in flames. The second missile struck the Kredmash factory, decimating the structure and leaving a large crater. Immediately following the attack, it was reported by western media that 1000 people were inside the mall, but from video evidence, this turned out to be a gross exaggeration typical of initial reports involving the war in Ukraine. The exaggeration led to allegations on social media that Ukraine was conducting a false flag operation. However, Russia took responsibility for the incident but insisted that they were targeting the factory, not the mall. Such an answer was not out of line with international standards as the US, Saudi Arabia, Israel, and countless other countries are given a pass to carry out these type of military actions targeting what they believe are military targets, irrespective of collateral damage. The governor of Poltava Oblast reported that 20 people were killed, while 56 people were injured. 36 people still remained unaccounted for. These numbers were a far cry from the 1000 initially reported to have possibly been injured or killed. Videos posted on social media showing the immediate aftermath of the missile strike when the mall caught fire, showed a minimal level of pedestrian traffic nowhere near indicative of 1000 people possibly being inside the mall at the time of the strike. The mistrust evoked by such exaggeration led to widespread skepticism as opposed to the large scale outcry that such a tragedy should evoke.

## Chapter 8: US Involvement and Hypocrisy

In mid-March, Russian troops fired a number of missiles at a military facility in Yavotiv, Lyiv Oblast, which is near the Ukraine/Polish border. The long range missiles that hit a military facility in Lyiv were said to come from warplanes operating over the Black Sea. Russia at the start of their invasion attempted to disrupt Ukrainian air defense by striking a number military and civilian targets using long range missiles. A number of them were fired from Belarus and struck the Zhytomyr Airport, which was a civilian airport. The absence of air support from the US allowed Russia to wipe out a significant number of Ukraine's air defense facilities. The US, however, on March 1st made sure to establish a line of control between them and the Russian forces for the sake of ensuring that escalation between the US and Russia would not occur. Despite the initial lack of support from the west, Ukraine managed to destroy Russian aircraft, 10 of them on March 5th. As of March 6th, Ukraine destroyed 88 Russian war planes since the start of the war on February 24th. As to why the US would not send fighter jets to Ukraine, the reason given, according to a US defense official, was that Ukraine still had a significant majority of its military aircraft. Despite US refusal to help in this regard, Ukraine's use of surface to air missiles, combined with Russia's lack of precision-guided capability, left Russian air forces having to fly and launch airstrikes at lower altitudes leaving themselves open to being struck down by surface to air missile launchers. Ukrainian soldiers were shooting Russian planes down with launchers that could be mounted on the shoulder. Another factor that slowed the Russian advance was the inexperience of its pilots.

When it came to Naval warfare, control of the Black Sea was a primary objective. Turkey, however, shortly after the start of Russia's invasion of Ukraine, blocked Russia's access through the Bosphorus and Dardanelles straits. This came four days after it was reported that a Russian warship attacked and took control of Snake Island. Ukraine was able to counter attack with the help of US intelligence helping them locate Russian warships using drones. Russia, in the meantime, was able to capture roughly twelve or so Ukrainian ships in Berdiansk, while Ukraine reported to have destroyed a Russian ship that docked there. During the month of March, the UN International Maritime Organization, in light of food shortages a result of Ukraine being unable to ship its grain, tried to set up a maritime corridor that would provide safe access for merchant vessels. Ukraine has already mined the sea area near its ports to repel Russian ships, but at the same time restricted their own ability to export goods.

Russia's main Black Sea vessel, Moskva, was destroyed and sunk by Ukraine's Neptune anti-ship cruise missiles. Both the US and Russia confirmed this. Russia, in response, fired missiles into Kyiv destroying the missile factory Luch Design Bureau, which was where the Neptune missiles were being manufactured. Nonetheless, Ukraine continued to resist the Russian naval assault and attempted to reclaim Snake Island in early May of 2022 and destroyed a Russian Serba-class landing craft operating in the Black Sea. They also fired a barrage of bombs on Snake Island where the Russian forces were.

One of the biggest scares of the Russian/Ukraine conflict was the possibility of Russia using tactical nuclear weapons in an act of desperation to appear victorious. In April, Russia began testing its Satan-2 missiles and threatened the US over its involvement in helping Ukraine. Because of Russia's lack of care during the assault on Zaporizhzhia and Chrenobyl which led to the nuclear plant catching fire at Zaporizhzhia after Russia fired missiles near its location, President Zelenskyy urged the international community to reassess whether Russia should be allowed to continue its development of nuclear resources. Zelenskyy urged for a consensus that Russia's nuclear supply be managed at the international level. This was followed by Germany sending tanks to Ukraine, to which after evoked more threats from Russia, threats which declared the possibility of a preemptive nuclear strike against nations aiding Ukraine during the war. Russia has the largest arsenal of nuclear weapons in the world. Russia's threats to use nuclear weapons led to the resignation of Boris Bondarev, a Russian diplomat.

Zelenskyy's decision to weaponize civilians against the Russian invasion was questioned in some media circles like the Washington Post, fearing it would escalate the damage. Many residents in Ukraine volunteered to fight for the Ukrainian defense force, while others made Molotov cocktails meant to be used against Russian forces. Civilians also knocked down Russian road signs in order to confuse Russian troops as to their exact location. There were also street protests against Russian forces occupying certain parts of Ukraine, which often escalated into physical and verbal violence. Some protesters were filming the Russian troops and recording their ID numbers. Other civilians began forming guerrilla units, which was encouraged by the Ukrainian defense forces. In response to civilian confrontation, Russian troops would fire their guns into the air or in some cases, in the direction of the protesters. Some of the demonstrators were detained and others executed. After residents began filming the location of Russian troops and equipment and sending them to Ukrainian forces for the sake of facilitating attacks, they became considered by the Russian forces as combatants actively taking part in hostilities. From there, things escalated quickly and Russian troops began going door to door in residential areas, confiscating cell phones and arresting people who took pictures of Russian tanks.

Both the United States and International Human Rights organizations have to take responsibility for this paradigm of unaccountably applied by countries ranked in the higher echelons of military capability. While historically, the enforcement of applying reprisals against nations in violation of human rights has been largely absent, the biggest error in this generation has not so much been in terms enforcing international regulations, but applying such standards in a uniform manner. The most egregious example of this is taking place now during the Russia/Ukraine war. International organizations have come out and initiated investigations into Russia's actions in Ukraine and called for other international organizations to follow suit, which was something largely absent during the US invasion of Iraq, both during and after, as many international human rights organizations such as the Human Rights Watch have only gone so far as to urge the United States to conduct internal investigations, despite knowing the fact that the US invasion of Iraq was illegal and unjustified. Whereas now, under similar circumstances, during the Russia/Ukraine war, international organizations have openly called for the international kommunity to investigate and prosecute Russia for war crimes. Unlike inquires into US war crimes in the middle east, where human rights investigators were sure to implicate both sides in terms of not doing enough to keep civilians safe from the crossfire, many perhaps with the exception of Amnesty International, have not investigated any role Ukrainian forces may have had in endangering the civilian population. This lack of thoroughness in applying the investigative process will give NATO and the US the green light to continue disregarding international human rights standards, and the international human rights organizations will have to take some of the blame for this. In order to circumvent this, Russia must re-establish a concordance with Amnesty International, whom has shown that it will conduct a thorough analysis when necessary. The importance of thorough analysis is for the protection of civilians in nations who do not support war, nor support fighting in it. This was clear during Russia's invasion of Ukraine since it was the case that many Ukrainian men were trying to leave the country, but were forced to stay and fight. Furthermore, during the Russia/Ukraine war, international organizations have failed to distinguish provocateurs—whose  only purpose for attending a peaceful public demonstration was to take actions that would only provoke unrest, from that of the ordinary civilian whose only objective was peace and life. Those demonstrators who went out and willfully engaged in hostilities with the occupiers in residential areas, thus endangering the civilian population, were never factored into the investigative framework, which justified, at least from the vantage point of human rights organizations, concluding that Russia ordered civilians to killed. Keep in mind that the international laws of war only apply from the commencement of hostilities, not the circumstances surrounding the decision to launch a military operation—whether justified or not.  Human Rights is not a new dynamic in world affairs. The concept has been around since the beginning of time. The enforcement, however, has never really held firm for any significant length of time. In many cases, justice for victims of war crimes could only be carried out on perpetrators after there was regime change in the country of the officials that were responsible for human rights violations. For example, if Germany was not defeated in World War II, there would have been no Nuremberg Trials to prosecute Nazi officials responsible for genocide and human rights violations. This is why many world powers are afraid of the ICC because essentially issuing an arrest warant for sitting government officials is ultimately a call for regime change, something which seperatist groups in many countries are eager to carry out. Historically, nations that were often more advanced and militarily adept were the ones that often carried out the most egregious violations of human rights. Germany and Japan slaughtered millions of civilians during World War II, while the US has carried out a vast number of war crimes in Iraq, the middle east, and Africa. In all three cases, the nations involved were considered the most civilized and advanced of their era. From 2003 to 2022, the United States, during their illegal occupation of Iraq, has carried out numerous violations of human rights such as conducting strikes on civilian population using high-powered explosives. There were rapes, torture, as well as mistreatment of prisoners, children, and refugees. Much of these allegations have been verified via direct footage, interviews with witnesses, Wikileaks reports, and compiled in a number of research works like the one published by Noor-ul-Ain Khawaja called Human Rights Violations Under US Occupation in Iraq: An Analysis.

Scores of civilians were killed by US forces during their occupation of Iraq. Some were killed by direct gunfire from US ground troops, others were killed by airstrikes conducted by the US Air Forces. Three of the most violent incidents concerning the mass murder of Iraqi civilians occurred in Fallujah, Haditha, and Nisour Square. Throughout the Iraq War, it has been documented that the US fired depleted uranium weapons into civilian areas, destroying infrastructure. It also been documented that the US has used cluster munitions, as well as white phosphorous. In addition, the US admitted, after numerous denials, that they have used napalm bombs, which is an incendiary substance banned by the United Nations for use in warfare since 1980. Wikileaks confirmed that the US had roughly 2836 chemical weapons as part of its arsenal in Iraq during the war. Russia during its invasion of Ukraine as of June 11th 2022 has not used any chemical weapons. CS gas which is banned for use in warfare was also used by the US during the Iraq war, which violated Article I of Convention on Chemical Weapons.

Depleted Uranium bombs were dropped via air strikes in Iraq on civilian areas by both US and UK forces, causing the air to fill up with intense radiation that can cause serious physiological problems like cancer, birth defects, gene damage and neurological problems. In the first year of the war between 2003 and 2004, according to a study published by the Lancet Journal, US forces killed roughly 100,000 civilians in Iraq, half being women and children. Most of the civilians killed died from airstrikes carried out by US-led forces. The study sampled 33 neighborhoods in Iraq that were most representative of the whole population, and concluded that the leading cause of the death had gone from mostly other typical causes like heart attack and stroke to overwhelmingly death as a result of violence. The study found that an Iraqi's the risk of death from military artillery and violence was astronomically higher than it was before the US invaded, 58 times higher in fact. The study was heavily peer-reviewed and edited and began to cast doubt on the US military's conduct during the war. It was led by Les Roberts from the John Hopkins Bloomberg School of Public Health who had around five doctors conduct interviews in 988 households, gathering data with a survey and putting themselves in danger during the process. The interviews compiled data given to them by members of the Iraqi households who reported the number of births and deaths in their family, both 14 months before and 14 months after the US invasion of their country. While some did not present death certificates, circumstances surrounding the information given in those cases, as well as the cultural backdrop was such that the interviewers ultimately considered that it was unlikely they were fabricating the information. The study showed that infant mortality rose, going from 29 deaths per 1000 births 14 months before the war, to 57 deaths per 1000 live births 14 months after the war started. This was attributed to women being unable to access hospitals during war, and thus having to deliver the baby without the sufficient medical supervision. The biggest increase was that of violent death, which the study attributed mostly to be caused by airstrikes, as opposed to hostility from ground forces. They did record three incidents of civilians being killed at checkpoints by gunfire from ground troops, which was minute compared to the devastation caused by airstrikes. The cases recorded which did involve direct fire from US troops involved the victim being mistaken for a combatant. The study documented that US troops did apologize directly to the families in those cases. The sample of 58 incidents of violent death recorded by the study were all caused by aerial strikes, the worst being in Fallujah, where 75% of the violent deaths took place, based on the sample. Much like the theater bombing in March of 2022 that Russia provided no information on in terms of number of casualties, the US forces in Iraq in the first year did not assess body count as well.

One of the first cases of the mass killing of Iraqi civilians carried out by US forces occurred in Fallujah. where civilians were killed en masse by US forces with airstrikes, gunfire, and chemical weapons between 2003 and 2005. According to some estimates, altogether during the US attack on Fallujah between 2003 and 2004, 6000 people were killed, mostly civilians which included women and children. There was photographic evidence which showed residents whose skin had been completely dissolved. A number of residents reported that US forces crushed the wounded by rolling over them with tanks, and they also reported that those looking to provide aid were shot. The Iraq Red crescent was not allowed into the city to provide aid and doctors were restricted from performing emergency surgeries on their patients. These were gross violations of the Geneva convention and many of these crimes perpetrated by US forces were documented in "Fallujah, The Hidden Massacre" which is a documentary film by Sigfrido Ranucci and Maurizio Torrealta.

The dynamic which led to the massacre in Fallujah is likely similar to how things escalated in Kyiv upon the Russian forces entering the city. Back in April of 2003, after the US Military during their unjustified occupation of Fallujah, no different than Russia's occupation of Kyiv, imposed a curfew for the residents living there, the residents protested. Just prior, the US forces had occupied a school and the residents of Fallujah wanted the troops to vacate the school so that it could reopen. Much like Russia's invasion of Ukraine in areas where Russian forces occupied certain parts without engaging in hostilities on the residents, the US forces in the case of their occupation of Fallujah did the same. In both cases, the occupying military force was eventually confronted by the residents living there. On April 28, 2003, roughly 200 Iraqi residents assembled outside the school where the US forces were stationed at the time. After the protesters became more and more agitated, US forces threw smoke into the crowd in order to repel them. When things escalated, according to the testimony of US forces, someone from the crowd sparked the violence when he opened fire on US soldiers, which caused US forces to return fire and ultimately kill 17 Iraqi civilians in the process. 70 others suffered serious wounds. Human Rights Watch later confirmed that no Iraqis had fired upon US soldiers during the confrontation. Two days later when protesters gathered outside of a US base at the former Ba'ath party headquarters, US forces shot 3 protesters and subsequently called in more reinforcements to Fallujah. In that case, the US also maintained that the protesters fired first. Meanwhile, seeing that things were escalating, US service members in Fallujah began going around confiscating motor bikes from Iraqi residents in the area, for the sake of mitigating the threat of terror against US military personnel. In June of 2003, residents-turned-insurgents in Fallujah began firing on US military in response to their unjustified invasion of the country, no different than Ukrainians in Kyiv against the Russian occupiers. In June, a US Service member was killed when the vehicle he was in was hit by an RPG round. Six other US military personnel sustained injuries. This led to heightened hostilities that would have dangerous implications for civilians in the area. In late June, a mosque was bombed, killing the imam and eight others. Residents accused the US of carrying out the bombing, but the US insisted it was the insurgents who did it by accident as they were making bombs nearby. Later in February 2004, insurgents had then started attacking US military convoys carrying high level US commanders, and firing upon them with RPGs from the rooftops in the surrounding areas. RPGs were also found in residential buildings in Mariupol in April of 2022 after the Russian siege of the city. Another similarity is how the US portrayed resistance to their invasion with how the Russian troops portrayed resistance to their invasion of Ukraine—the US relegated those resisting their invasion to being insurgents linked to Al-Qaeda, while Russia considered those resisting their invasion as belonging to Neo-Nazi groups. Following the attacks on US servicemen in Iraq, Fallujah was quickly consumed by a strong guerrilla presence which endangered civilians there. This guerrilla aspect in Kyiv and other parts of Ukraine during the Russian invasion in 2022 was strongly encouraged by Ukrainian officials. This leads one to ask if this was wise, and whether or not the Ukrainians are more justified to attack occupying forces than the Iraqis were in Fallujah back in 2004 when the US launched an unjustified invasion of their country. We can see the difference in western media's coverage of the two events. The resistors to US occupation in Iraq were seen as terrorists, while the resistors in Ukraine to Russian occupiers are viewed as freedom fighters.

Due to the rising guerrilla warfare in Fallujah against US troops, US forces had to briefly withdraw in March of 2004, leaving only a few personnel to reassert foothold over the city every now and then. However, after five members of a combat engineer team—sent out to ensure a safe passage route for the US 82$^{nd}$ Airborne and Blackwater forces—were killed by a roadside bomb on their way to Fallujah, the nature of the operations became set to change considerably. This was followed by the killing of four armed US contractors traveling in their SUV to make a delivery to food services. They were hit by insurgent gunfire before being decimated with a grenade that insurgent threw into their SUV. This was followed by a mob who set the bodies of the contractors on fire before dragging them through the streets and hanging them over a bridge at the Euphrates. Thus, all the civilian friendly strategies applied by the US after their initial advance into Fallujah had to be abandoned, and US forces would then be ordered to conduct a more full scale assault to clear out the guerrillas. It is likely that the Russian forces followed a similar dynamic in many parts of Ukraine. Also interesting to note is that the US would call this offensive aimed at clearing out the guerrillas, a "pacification" of the city. Somewhat similar to how Russian President Putin called his military operation in Ukraine a "denazification,"

On April 1$^{st}$ 2004, The US began a major assault on Fallujah, launching air strikes that destroyed four residential homes. On the 5$^{th}$ of April, US forces imposed a curfews to all residents and encouraged them to help them identify the perpetrators of the Blackwater killings. *(Russian troops in Bucha asked residents there to help them find the nazis)* The bombing raids subsequently carried out by US forces killed numerous insurgents as well as civilians. It had been estimated that just in the first few days of April of 2004, 300 Iraqi civilians had been killed. By the beginning of May, it was estimated that close to 600 civilians were killed during that first battle at Fallujah.

The second battle at Fallujah(Operation Phantom Fury) started in November of 2004 and lasted until December 24, 2004. During this operation, US forces went door to door looking for insurgents, very similar to how the Russians went door to door in

Bucha looking for Nazis. In the 2005 documentary, "Fallujah, The Hidden Massacre." a former US soldiers named Jeff Englehart, who was deployed to Fallujah at the time, revealed that he was told that every one walking outside was an enemy combatant. *(This is also likely what happened in Bucha—Russian troops were told that anyone walking outside was an enemy combatant)* Another US soldier, Ross Caputi, who fought during the battle recounted tactics that involved firing indiscriminately into residential homes before seeing who was inside, for fear that there could be insurgents there. This is exactly similar to the tactic used by the Russian forces in Bucha, as witnessed by one of the residents there. In both cases of Iraq and Bucha, civilians were killed in the process. Caputi, in an interview with CNN, said that "These tactics were meant to keep us safe. But I learned later that tens of thousands of civilians were still hiding in their houses during the operation, so these tactics would have put them in a lot of danger. ...The hardship that Phantom Fury imposed on Fallujans and the destruction it caused made me feel really ashamed of what we were doing." According to the Red Cross, 800 civilians were killed during the battle, while Iraqi non-profit groups estimated that close to 6000 Iraqi civilians were killed.

Another massacre that occurred during the US invasion of Iraq was the Haditha massacre which killed 24 Iraqi civilians. It occurred on November 19, 2005 when a group of US Marines carried out summary executions of men, women, children, and the elderly, all shot at point blank range. The motive was said to be in response to the killing of Lance Corporal Miguel Terrazas who was killed during an IED attack on a US Marine convoy. After the incident, a false report was filed stating that the explosion killed 15 civilians, while eight insurgents were killed as the Marines subsequently opened fire. After an investigation carried out by the Pentagon which showed substantial evidence that the Marines carried out summary executions of Iraqi civilians, those involved in the massacre were later indicted on charges of murder. However, in 2008, only one Marine was penalized for the crimes. The others had the charges dropped. The one penalized who had to stand trial was only given a demotion in rank as part of a plea deal in 2012 in which the murder charged would be dropped. No one was jailed and no justice was granted to the victims.

Prior to the massacre, US forces were present around Haditha for the purpose of keeping watch over a Dam that provided hydroelectric power. There had been numerous flare ups of insurgent violence since the start of the war, as insurgents against occupation attacked US troops regularly in that area. When a convoy of US Marines was attacked via roadside bomb placed along their route in 2005, one of the US servicemen driving one of the vehicles in the convoy was killed. The other two present in the vehicle with him suffered serious injuries, but survived. One of them was allowed to return to active duty.

Immediately following the attack, other members of the convoy began a furious assault on civilians in the area. One Iraqi man and four Iraqi teenagers who were in a white taxi cab near the attack were forced out and shot dead by Staff Sgt Frank Wuterich. According to two Iraqi soldiers and a Marine, they had been forced to stand in a line outside the taxi cab with their hands up before being shot and killed by Wuterich, who later said that he felt threatened by them. The Marines reported to have heard gunfire coming from all sides, and suspected some of it to be coming from behind the white taxi as it drove up near the area. Another Marine, Sgt. Sanick Dela Cruz, present at the time told investigators that after Staff Sgt. Wuterich opened fire on the victims, he (Dela Cruz) then urinated on their dead bodies out of anger for what happened to Terrazas(the driver that was killed by the IED). Dela Cruz was also forthright about the clear intent to kill civilians, telling investigators: "As I crossed the median I saw one of the Iraqi civilians, who was standing in the center of the line, drop to the ground.....Immediately afterwards another Iraqi standing by him raised his hands to his head. I then heard other small arms fire and looked to my left and saw Sgt. Wuterich kneeling on one knee and shooting his M16 in the direction of the Iraqi civilians."

When another Marine, Lieutenant William Kallop, the platoon commander, arrived on the scene, he reported that they encountered gun fire coming from one of the residential homes nearby shortly after the IED attack. In response, after Cpl Hector A. Salinas said he could see someone was firing the shots on the south part of the road, Kallop ordered Staff Sgt Wuterich to move into area and "clear south". Using tactics of first throwing grenades and firing indiscriminately into the houses before entering, Wuterich and three other Marines, Salinas, Tatum and Lance Cpl. Humberto M. Mendoza, ended up killing 19 more civilians in the process, seven of which were children. At the first home that the US soldiers engaged, they tried to enter via the kitchen, Tatum reported to investigators that he thought he heard what sounded like an AK-47 being set to open fire, so he threw grenades into the home. A 37 year old man named Walid Hasan, who was inside the home, was killed. And so was 66 year old Khamisa Ali, who was killed in the hallway area. Four more in the home at the time were killed by grenades and gunfire. The nine year old girl living there whose name was Iman Walid Abdul-Hamid said that the Marines were shooting into all the rooms of the house. After they killed the civilians in the first house, the Marines rushed into the second house believing that the suspected gunman fled there. Mendoza told investigators that the same protocol used on the first house was applied to the second home. He also admitted to killing 43 year old Yunis Rasif through the kitchen door. When the Marines entered the house, they went to the bedroom and before looking inside they threw grenades in the room and opened fire into it, killing all the women and children inside. Despite carrying out the slaughter, Tatum insisted that he felt threatened at the time and that he was simply reacting based on that fear, telling investigators that he did not fire with the intent to kill civilians. One can presume that the Russians who carried out the exact same mode of operation in Bucha will likely say the same thing, which will put international war crimes investigators on the spot when they have to explain the difference between the massacre at Haditha and the massacre at Bucha. It was later revealed that Marines had gone to a 3rd and 4th house, after seeing men who were staring at them suspiciously. According to some Iraqi witnesses, the Marines separated the men from the women at the homes before forcing the men into the fourth house and executing them.

According to Wuterich, it was standard protocol to fire into buildings deemed hostile and that he was only following orders based on that. Marines were not required to risk their lives by identifying individual targets as threats when a structure is deemed hostile. Kallop testified that "Once you declare a building hostile, you can destroy it with all means at your disposal." It is likely that the Russian military has this same policy.

There was a lot of criticism against the US military because they only responded to the allegations of Marines killing civilians in Haditha after Time magazine began reporting about the incident. Initially, US Marine officials felt the incident was no different than other situations in which civilian casualties occurred. Maj. Gen. Richard A. Huck believed that the allegations were lies perpetrated by the insurgents in order smear the reputation of the US military. Compare that to Russia's initial reaction to allegations of war crimes committed by Russian soldiers in Bucha, when Russian officials insisted that the incident was staged. In the case of the Haditha massacre, other Marine officers insisted that their men were not murderers. Many in the Kremlin likely have this same sentiment about their own soldiers.

In terms of allegations that Marine officers were attempting to cover up the incident, Dela Cruz told investigators that Staff Sgt Wuterich asked him to support reports that the men from the taxi were trying to escape, but those investors on the scene saw no evidence that a large scale cover-up was attempted.

In December of 2006, the US Military charged Frank Wuterich, Sanick P. Dela Cruz, James Donahue and Stephen Tatum with unpremeditated murder. Frank Wuterick had been charged with 12 counts of unpremeditated murder. Even after it was concluded that there were no weapons in the taxi nor insurgents in the first two houses that came under attack, all charges were dropped against the Marines in 2008. Wuterich who was the only one to face a trial, was allowed a plea deal in 2012 to plead guilty to dereliction of duty and receive a fine and a penalty of demotion in rank, while charges of manslaughter would be dropped. The lack of disciplinary action by US military in connection to the Haditha massacre enabled other acts of violence against civilians to be carried out with impunity. Similar atrocities occurred later in Ishaqi near Balad, Qaim, Taal Al Jal, Mukaradeeb, Hamdaniyah, Samarra and Salahuddin. Amnesty International reported in 2011 that the number of civilian killed individually by US forces between 2004 and 2009 totaled around 66,000.

Another massacre carried out by US troops in Iraq was at Nisour Square in Baghdad when guards from the BlackWater group, a US security contractor, shot and killed 17 unarmed civilians, including a nine year old boy. All who stood trial in connection with the incident were either acquitted or eventually pardoned by the President of the United States. The incident took place on September 16, 2007 when BlackWater Security Consulting employees responded to reports of an explosion near where US and Iraqi officials were conferencing. A tactical unit in a convoy of 4 trucks consisting of 19 Blackwater employees arrived on the scene and got into formation on the south side of Nisour Square to provide safe evacuation passage for US officials as well as other BlackWater employees protecting them. Shortly thereafter, when a car was seen driving towards them, the unit began firing at civilians, killing 17 of them in the process. Later, during trial in 2014, the BlackWater employees said they believed that the approaching car was a hostile threat and thus began shooting in the name of self-defense. The car, a Kia sedan, was later destroyed with a grenade. Iraqi government officials and US Military officials had different accounts of the incident. The Iraqi government reported that the approaching car was inhabited by a woman and her adult son. They were driving on the wrong side of the road and ignored the police whistle to allow the convoy of BlackWater employees to pass thru. Subsequently, after firing a warning shot, the BlackWater team, as well as its helicopters, opened fire on the car killing the woman and her adult son. When the team threw stun grenades to clear the area, Iraqi police and soldiers mistook it from frag grenades and then began firing at the BlackWater team, which led to BlackWater employees opening fire.

The US Military account of the incident reported that the approaching car was ignoring all warnings being given which led BlackWater employees to shoot at the car. When Iraqi police attempted go and help the passengers inside the vehicle, the BlackWater employees were under the impression that the Iraqi policemen were trying to push the car towards the BlackWater unit, which led to Blackwater employees believing that it was a car bomb, to which caused them to open fire at the car, killing both the passengers and the Iraqi policemen. Immediately after, other Iraqi police began to fire upon the BlackWater unit.

According to a New York Times report in 2007, one of the BlackWater employees during the chaos continued to fire in the direction of civilians, even after ceasefire was ordered. And later, three BlackWater guards said that they believed that the shootings were not justified. A joint American-Iraqi investigation ensued and found that BlackWater was responsible for the killing of 17 unarmed Iraqi civilians after opening fire without provocation. An October 2007 US military report concluded that none of the Iraqi police or soldiers fired back at the BlackWater guards. The UN considered the BlackWater contractors as "mercenaries" and in violation of the international law. Criminal charges of 14 counts of manslaughter were filed against five BlackWater employees, but despite conclusive evidence, a U.S. judge dropped all charges against the BlackWater security firm in 2010. In 2011, the charges were reinstated by a federal appeals court panel, and in 2013, the charges for one of the accused were dropped. The rest went to trial in 2014 and were found guilty. One was given a life sentence, while the other three were to serve 30 years in prison. In 2020, all four were granted an official presidential pardon by the President of the United States and released from prison. The UN Human Rights Office warned that such would only enable other entities to carry out similar crimes with impunity.

BlackWater not only got away with the Nisour Square massacre, but others violent incidents that transpired prior to it. A year before in 2006, a BlackWater sniper opened fire from the roof of the building belonging to the Iraqi Justice Ministry and killed three civilians. The incident was deemed justified and an act of self-defense. In December of 2006, a Black Water employee killed the bodyguard of Iraq's Vice President, but suffered no legal reprisals.

The International Committee of the Red Cross (ICRC) reported in 2004 that the occupying forces were responsible for enforced disappearances after arresting and detaining certain individuals in Iraq, not telling the family where they were taken. Just within the city of Fallujah, 280 persons were declared missing, all confirmed by name and picture ID.

Rapes and murders were also perpetrated by US soldiers in Iraq. In 2006, a group of US servicemen who were all intoxicated and wearing regular clothes and masks, invaded a home where an Iraqi family was residing. One of the soldiers assumed the role of standing guard at the checkpoint to keep a look out for anyone else that could be in the area. After the US soldiers, broke into the home, they all raped a 14 year old girl named Abeer Kassem Hamza al-Janabi, while killing her mother, father, and sister.

After they finished raping the girl, they shot her dead as well, cracked her skull and then incinerated her body. However, in this case, the US did investigate and prosecute all involved. The families of the victims, however, expected a more harsh penalty such as the death penalty. Before the investigation, the incident was covered up by the perpetrators who tried to blame the act on Sunni insurgents.

After Russia's invasion of Ukraine on February 24, 2022, the US had called upon the International Criminal Court to prosecute Russia for war crimes committed in Ukraine. The declaration evoked charges from the public that the United States were hypocrites for encouraging an ICC investigation into Russia's actions in Ukraine, while blocking the ICC from investigating their crimes in Afghanistan, where US airstrikes killed scores of civilians. The US does not recognize the jurisdiction of the International Criminal Court, which was first formed in 1998 through an international consensus called the Rome Statue. Back then, the US helped facilitate the agreement and initial formation of the ICC, but refused to officially join for fear that the prosecutor for the ICC would wield an enormous level of influence and power, possibly conducting investigations based on political affiliation. Discourse about the establishment of an international treaty dealing with war crimes was prevalent in political circles after the Nuremberg Trials, and Congress during the decade of the 1990s approved a number of resolutions that urged for an international investigative body. When the US became concerned about the level of power the ICC could wield, they ended up voting against the Rome Statue. Russia also does not recognize the jurisdiction of the ICC, but nonetheless the ICC is conducting investigations into Russia's actions in Ukraine and whether or not they constitute war crimes. Meanwhile, the US is encouraging the ICC to carry on, even while not recognizing ICC jurisdiction for fear of opening itself up to being investigated for war crimes in the middle east. Still and all, if the US wanted to get involved in prosecuting Russia, they would have to navigate around US legislation which largely prohibits the US from cooperating with the ICC. But the US supports ICC investigation into crimes that are not being investigated by the nation accused. The US has investigated a number of its own war crimes, but in most significant incidents, the suspects had the charges dropped or were acquitted. Russia may follow suit and conduct investigations into what occurred in Bucha and Mariupol and simply either drop the charges against the accused Russian soldiers or carry out a light sentence followed by a presidential pardon. As a side note, the US did support the ICC's investigation of genocide in Sudan during the Bush administration.

The US fear of the ICC conducting investigations based on a political motive ironically worked out in favor of the US when it came to Afghanistan. The ICC decided in October of 2021 to conduct a probe into the war crimes committed by the Taliban and ISIS-k, and at the same time scale down its investigation into crimes committed by the US and its allies in Afghanistan. The UK non-profit group Airwars estimated that US airstrikes killed between 22,000 and 48,000 civilians in Afghanistan, Iraq, and Syria and other major conflict zones in the middle east and Africa between 2001 and 2020. Regardless of that statistic, just as an investigation by the ICC into crimes committed by all parties in Afghanistan since 2003 was getting ready to start, the probe was suddenly suspended because the crimes committed by the Taliban and ISIS-k were considered by the ICC to be more egregious than those carried out by the US and its allies. The decision ultimately hurt the credibility of the ICC and made it appear as though the court has a western bias and is simply an instrument of the west. On top of that, the ICC has opened inquiries into war crimes committed by Russia and Israel, but largely looked the other way when it came to war crimes carried out by US and UK forces in Iraq and Afghanistan. This, despite the fact that the US has been very hostile towards the ICC, excoriating them for attempting to not only investigate the US for war crimes, but also for launching investigations into the military actions carried out by its ally Israel. Both nations insist that they never intended to target civilians, which is why Israel is all the more critical of the moral equivalence insinuated by ICC inquiries into Israel's activities in Palestinian territories-- Hamas, one of Israel's main adversaries, fires rockets directly at civilians with the intent to kill civilians, all of which is obvious to the human eye as videos capture rockets being fired en masse from Gaza into Israeli territory. Were it not for the Iron Dome, millions more in both Israel and Gaza would have perished. Human rights organizations, however, have insisted that war crimes by one nation during a conflict does not justify war crimes by the other.

Moreover, when it comes to US suspicions of the ICC, suspicions that the prosecutor could be swayed by politics, the actual instance of such happening worked out in favor of the US, not against it. The ICC decision not to fully investigate the US for war crimes was right on the heels of the US drone strike that killed an Afghan family of ten. Many believe had the New York Times not reported it, the US would have kept the incident under wraps.

The ICC started its operations in 2002 just after the US invaded Afghanistan, one of the nations that voted for the Rome Statue, a treaty that initiated the ICC. Afghanistan had been mired in war for years, starting back in the 70s when the Soviets occupied the country to protect that Afghan communist government there. It was estimated that over a million Afghans were killed during that time. This was followed by another violent conflict between the Taliban and the Northern Alliance in the years leading up to 9/11. Shortly after the ICC operations had gone into effect, the US immediately passed legislation to protect itself from international war crimes investigation and prosecution, as well as set up agreements with other countries in which they would also refuse to recognize the jurisdiction of the court. Most of the ICC's crackdown on war crimes were initially in Africa, but after public pressure, they began probing such cases outside of Africa and began a preliminary investigation into war crimes that took place in Afghanistan after 2002 when the ICC first began its operations. Many were beginning to believe that the ICC feared superpower nations. The ICC can investigate war crimes if one of the member nations calls for an investigation. They can also investigate in places that are referred to them by the UN Security Council. The third process by which ICC investigations can be initiated is when suspected war crimes occur in the nation of one of its member countries. Such was the case for the ICC attempt to launch a probe in Afghanistan. The US officials, however, have always insisted that its refusal to recognize the jurisdiction of the ICC was a bipartisan consensus. This served to stall the process, and when in 2017, the ICC began taking strong measures to get the court to grant permission to the ICC to investigate US crimes in Afghanistan, the pretrial chamber that was in charge of granting authorization to investigate prohibited the ICC from conducting the probe. It was clear that the decision was motivated as a result of pressure and intimidation from US officials. The national security advisor to the US president advised the president to impose sanctions against ICC officials as well as prohibit them from entering the US if they try to move forward with a probe. Despite the threats, the ICC did initially move forward with the Afghanistan investigation in March of 2020, which led to the US president imposing sanctions on two officials of the ICC. The US also threatened to prosecute ICC officials in US courts if they tried to bring charges against Americans. This was followed by US pressure on the US-backed Afghan government to oppose the ICC investigation and launch its own investigation in order to stifle the ICC probe. The ICC usually acquiesces to the policies within the nation state, and thus halted their Afghanistan probe, as well as the probe into CIA black sites which were secret prisons in Lithuania, Poland, and Romania where tortures allegedly took place. The culture of impunity largely fostered by the ICC in succumbing to US pressure gives way to and emboldens other nations to act without regard for consequences or condemnation. The ICC attempted to justify their decision to downscale the war crimes investigation by citing the heinousness of crimes carried out by ISIS-k and the Taliban against Afghan civilians, stating that their crimes warranted for greater resources to be applied to an investigation of their actions, as opposed to one that probes US actions in Afghanistan. Many consider US officials as hypocritical in their condemnation of Russia for invading Ukraine when they themselves actively subverted attempts by the ICC to hold them accountable for atrocities identical to the ones carried out by the Russian forces in Ukraine. Little to no international condemnation of the US for their crimes in the middle east is likely one of the factors that emboldened Russia to assert their geopolitical interests with impunity as well, giving credence to "might" essentially making "right."

The ICC has attempted to make up for their shortcomings in condemning superpowers like the United States by immediately attempting to open a probe into Russia's actions in Ukraine just days after Russia's invasion of the country on February 24, 2022. But this action on the part of the ICC was not met with respect, at least not from the non-western areas of the world. It was followed up with even more indignation from victims of US atrocities in the middle east and Africa in regards to how the US was being allowed to get away with crimes that the ICC is seeking to prosecute Russia for. One can presume that the ICC and other human rights organizations are not simply pro-western, but more along the lines of pro-western media. At the moment, the western media in recent years has for the most part taken a contrarian stance to GOP politics in America, due to the election of Donald Trump in 2016. In an effort to alleviate embarrasment and distance themselves from the movement that Trump had surrounding him at that time, the media would often side against any perspective they felt was upheld by the conservative outlook. Since 2016, it was heavily perceived that the GOP was both pro-Russian and pro-Israel. Donald Trump, during his tenure, was both open about his admiration of Russian President Putin and open about his support for the state of Israel. However, back in 2017, when President Trump approved sending lethal military aid to Ukraine in a move that didn't fit the Trump/pro-Russia narrative, western media agencies like Reuters condemned it. They published an article in 2017 disapproving of the decision to arm Ukraine. The commentary by Daniel DePetris was entitled "Why the U.S. shouldn't send arms to Ukraine." There were also many reports among western media that Ukraine had a neo-nazi problem. But after 2019, when the quid-pro-quo scandal occurred with Trump threatening to cut off lethal aid to Ukraine, the media shifted their stance on Ukraine in order to remain contrary to the GOP. The conrarianism was also applied by western media stance on Israel. Prior to Trump, the western media was heavily pro-Israel, but after 2017 when Trump recognized Jerusalem as Israel's capital, the western media began to shift against Israel. Ultimately, the contrarianism would set the left-leaning media against Russia and Israel, leading to human rights organizations following suit. In 2021, following the Gaza War, the media largely blamed Israel for the conflict, while UN human rights groups would create a commission which placed responsibility for the Gaza conflict on Israel's treatment of Palestinians, and not Hamas's insistence on firing rockets willfully and indiscriminately into Israeli territories. The ICC is also attempting to launch a war crimes probe into Israel's military operations. This goes to show how powerful the media is when it comes to not only controlling the narrative, but also in getting the international community to follow along. Furthermore, we can see how the media's support of democratic principles has shielded the US from any war crimes investigation, seeing that as of 2021, the US administration is led by a democratic head of state.

## Chapter 9: Amnesty International

After Russia shut down the Amnesty International Moscow office in April of 2022, the human rights organization became somewhat less impartial in their investigation of atrocities in Ukraine. Amnesty had a history of pointing out the necessity for both sides of the conflict to operate in a way that keeps the civilian population out of danger. But when Amnesty International released their Khariv report "ANYONE CAN DIE AT ANY TIME: Indiscriminate attacks by Russian forces in Kharkiv, Ukraine", it was clear that their approach had become one that nearly absolved Ukrainian forces from actions on their part which endangered and killed civilians, despite Amnesty documenting in that same report that Ukrainian forces were indeed deploying into residential areas as well as firing artillery from there. In addition, the report only documented civilians killed or injured by Russian artillery fired into residential neighborhoods. There were no reports of civilians killed by Ukrainian artillery, despite the same report admitting that Ukrainian forces were firing on Russian forces from residential areas. The report also only applied condemnation towards Russia for the use of cluster bombs even as the report basically insinuated that Ukrainian forces used them as well. This approach by human rights organizations in not keeping civilians out of and distinct from the framework of military conflict and crossfire hurts their credibility and questions the need for them since by doing this, they only serve as the propaganda arm for military forces. There are times when the perpetrator is obvious and can be singled out, but in some reports documenting evidence in which it is clear that both sides are endangering the civilian population, the organization reporting the incidents still, in this case, manages to place the responsibility only on one party. In the first few years following 9/11 when the US was considered to within their right to enact justice for the victims of 9/11 by invading Afghanistan, no one and no organization would have dared at that time questioned the actions of US forces. This lack of objectivity and impartiality on observing what was happening on the military front allowed the US to act with impunity and also guilt trip anyone who would dare question them. But after their indignation was complete, scores of innocent civilians have been killed, and now after the fact in hindsight, people are now alert to something they should have been vigilant about from the start. It may have saved innocent lives. Just observe how successful the diplomatic process was during the Donbas conflict prior to 2022 when consistent engagement by France and Germany, as well as human rights organizations' willingness to point out when both sides of the conflict were endangering civilian lives led to an agreement between both sides of the conflict which set in motion a natural process in which the breakaway regions would have slowly been reintegrated back into Ukraine. But now, as of 2022, the new manner of approach which downplays wrongdoing by one side will further polarize both parties in the conflict and stifle the potential of both Ukraine and Russia coming to a consensus. The moment either side feel as though they are no longer being watched, the atrocities will ensue. Prisoners will be tortured, and civilians will be rounded up at a far greater rate than has happened thus far during the war.

Kharkiv, like Mariupol and Bucha, was engulfed by intense shelling starting from February 24, 2022. Kharkiv was one of the areas of Eastern Ukraine that was nearly taken over by pro-Russian separatists back in 2014. At the time, most of Kharkiv was pro-Russian, and after Crimea joined the Russian Federation, a group of separatists in Kharkiv wanted to establish a KPR(Kharkiv People's Republic), but were stifled by Ukrainian security forces and pro-Ukrainian officials in the region. Despite Ukraine keeping Kharkiv from becoming a breakaway region like Donetsk and Luhansk, unrest still occurred in 2014 and 2015. There were shootings and bombings which killed people, both pro-Ukrainian and pro-Russian. But over the years leading up to Russia's full scale invasion, Kharkiv was coming to terms with the pro-western Ukrainian movement. This in effect led many who lived in Kharkiv to adopt a neutral political outlook, keeping their Russian nationalism in check. After the separatist attempt to take over Kharkiv was stopped by Ukrainian forces, the city had come under the control of the SBU, the Security Service of Ukraine, a police agency that has carried out extrajudicial killings against pro-Russian citizens.

Back in March of 2014, violent confrontation occurred in Kharkiv between pro-Russian groups and Ukrainian nationalists and led to the killing of two pro-Russian demonstrators during the clashes. While much of the population, both pro-Ukrainian and pro-Russian, tried to steer clear of the hostilities, they were nonetheless influenced by the unrest and divided politically as a result. The pro-Russian activists declared the KPR on April 6th 2014, not long after the DPR was established in Donetsk. Shortly thereafter, however, their attempt at autonomy was destroyed by Ukrainian security forces when they forced the pro-Russian activists out of the regional administration building. Still and all, pro-Russian groups continued to fight the Ukrainian forces through other methods of terrorism. The Ukrainian Security Service uncovered and stopped 39 terrorist acts from occurring. Despite the vigilance by Ukrainian authorities, pro-Russian terrorists in February of 2015 set off an IED at Euromaindan march for Euromaidan victims, killing 4 people in the process. The sporadic violence continued, and several combatants engaged in gun battles. Many explosions which occurred in the region as a result of storing ammunition were attributed to acts of sabotage carried out by terrorists. An explosion in Balaklia killed two people, and damaged 300 homes. Amid the incidents of violence in Kharkiv, it had nonetheless become the designated refuge for those displaced by the war in Donbas. It was estimated that close to 400,000 people ended up in Kharkiv, which placed a huge burden on the economy and hospitals. Not to mention, some of the displaced were not welcomed with open arms due to the strain their presence put on the cost of living and access to social services. Many could not afford to pay rent and at the same time, could not secure a job that could keep up with the standard of living.

A number of human rights groups have documented the actions taken by the Ukrainian Security Service (SBU) against pro-Russian activists, actions that involved extrajudicial violence. Between 2014 and 2018, 1000 people are arrested and held over incidents stemming from the unrest and separatism taking place throughout eastern Ukraine. The constant threat of terror led to some human rights violations on the part of the SBU. A number of these violations which were documented by human rights groups included enforced disappearances and torture. There has also during this time been a lack of initiative on the part of Ukraine to uphold accountability for crimes perpetrated by far right groups that often attacked the LGBT community. There had also been no move towards acquiring justice for the victims of the violence in

Kharkiv whom were simply caught in the middle of hostilities between far right groups and separatists. And much like Kharkiv, there had also been no justice for the victims in the Odessa tragedy where pro-Ukrainian groups in May of 2014 set fire to the House of Trade Unions where pro-Russian activists barricaded themselves in refuge from the pro-Ukrainian groups shortly after clashes near the city center. Forty-two pro-Russian activists, which included 7 women and a boy, died in the fire as local police and late-arriving fire-fighters did little to protect them. Odessa has been another case of how western bias on the part of human rights organizations enabled impunity to prevail.

In Kharkiv, prior to the Russian invasion, recovery from the Euromaidan unrest and pro-Russian separatism was largely slowed by favoritism and political pressure, which oftentimes manifested at the legal level in cases where the defendants would be acquitted and saved from facing punishment for crimes against political opposition. Accountability was still largely neglected there, and while many pro-Russian groups began to assert neutrality, the tensions regarding Ukraine's lack of initiative to bring justice to victims of ethnic clashes allowed much of the hostility to fester, albeit in many cases, quietly. A number of allegations against Ukraine regarding the treatment of pro-Russian activists were never investigated. Such as the allegation about secret prisons in Kharkiv where political opponents would secretly be detained without anyone knowing of their whereabouts over a two year period. However, both the pro-Russian and pro-Ukrainian element in the administrative and judicial sector has played a role in suppressing adequate accountability. For example, Nelia Shtepa was on trial on charges of separatism/terrorism, but since the judges who may have leaned along a similar political framework as the defendant, took every effort to avoid taking up the case due to political pressure to ensure her conviction, no justice would be end up being served there. Another example is how when former mayor of Kharkiv Gennady Kernes, a pro-Russian separatist turned pro-Ukrainian, was charged with kidnapping and torture of two Euromaidan activists, he ultimately was set free due to prosecutors not attending any of the hearings, which led to the case being dropped. And this was largely for political reasons. This problem in Ukrainian politics is a major reason why President Zelenskyy was so popular in Ukraine and won the presidential election in 2019 in a landslide. One of his goals was to fix this issue of corruption in the judicial system. Zelenskyy was also very keen on healing the rift between Russian-speakers and Ukrainian speakers in Ukraine.

The post Euromaidan/pre-Russian invasion era had also seen a largely unchecked police force operate in a way that intimidated political activists with tactics such as labeling and torture, which much of Kharkiv had come to tolerate. This led many of the pro-Russian elements in Kharkiv to drift over to the fringes. Regardless, despite the backdrop of Euromaidan fueled unrest, only 7% of the population there supported being integrated into Russia, according to a poll from 2017. Kharkiv's importance to Russia is heavily motivated by its past. Kharkiv was basically the Silicon Valley for the Soviet Union, a legacy left largely intact after the USSR's collapse. Sporting a metropolis with some impressive skyscrapers, prior to the Russian invasion the city, and much like Silicon Valley, Kharkiv cultivated many highly skilled and technical IT experts, but of whom would usually leave the city to work elsewhere. Even before the Soviet Union, Kharkiv was established as a result of the treaty of Pereyaslav between Russia and Bohdan Khmelnytsky, the founder of Ukraine. The treaty made the country a protectorate of Russia in 1654. Subsequently, it became the major Ukrainian industrial center of the Russian empire and at one point was the capital of the Ukrainian Soviet Socialist Republic. Despite the rich legacy, it was also the place where some of the greatest atrocities of the Holodomor took place in the 1930s.

Right at the outset of Russia's invasion of Ukraine, the Russian troops began a massive assault on Kharkiv, shelling civilian areas regularly throughout the campaign. As a result, hundreds of civilians have been killed as Russian troops used cluster bombs to destroy many structures in residential areas. Amnesty International has documented that Ukrainian forces were also firing from residential areas, and may have been using cluster bombs as well. Russian forces initially laid siege to Kharkiv with an air and ground assault along with rocket strikes, but Ukrainian forces were able to resist the first advance of Russian forces there, steadily pushing the Russians back. However, the fierce shelling continued to ravage residential areas as of April 30th. A woman named Oksana was gravely wounded while walking in a park with her husband and daughter as a cluster bomb exploded nearby at the playground. The event completely transfigured their lives, as well as many others in Kharkiv. Oksana later died in June. The local director of  Kharkiv's Regional Military Administration confirmed that roughly 600 non-combatants had been killed from the start of the war in late February until late April. The governor of Kharkiv reported that 600 residential homes were destroyed by Russian artillery by mid March. Amnesty International between April and May investigated sites in Kharkiv where 60 civilians were killed as a result of being in areas that were hit by Russian artillery. They also had weapons technicians on hand to identify the type of fragments collected and which weapons they came from. A number of these fragments turned out to be from the aftermath of bombings in which cluster munitions were used. The use of land mines were also prevalent in the area, and so were grad rockets. It was concluded that these strikes by Russian forces were indiscriminate and took place between late February and late April, causing hundreds of thousands of civilians to flee. The governor estimated the number to be somewhere around 600,000. Those who remained were told to get into shelters that contained a basement, many of which were located in subways and schools. Amnesty International pointed out that repeated use of unguided missiles even when knowing in advance that they could cause civilian casualties is a war crime in itself.

Russia was never able to gain a foothold over the city due to strong Ukrainian resistance. They tried in late February and early March, but were repeatedly driven back and left having to rely on aerial and artillery bombardments. The shelling would subside by early May as Russian forces continued to retreat and prepare for a counter offensive. Meanwhile, Ukrainian forces were able to reclaim some of the areas previously under Russian control. While on the retreat, Russian forces continued bombarding Ukrainian neighborhoods with artillery strikes and cluster bombs, which are banned by international law. On Myru Street, nine Ukrainian civilians were killed by Russian strikes. In one of the victims hurt there, doctors found fragments from munition strikes. Many of the victims had been located in areas near the strikes such as in parks and courtyards. One woman, Tetiana Ahayeva, had come out of her basement to get some air before shortly encountering a cluster bomb explosion nearby. The neighbor's son would be killed instantly as a result of the explosion, and his father suffered severe wounds from the shrapnel. Tetiana's own son was wounded in the stomach by cluster munition pellets.

Bohdan Burlutsky, who lived nearby, was in his car when cluster bombs exploded at a courtyard near a residential building. Instantly, a number of cars were ablaze and he and many others were injured. Some people were killed. This attack occurred on Myru Street. Not far from there, a woman named Olha Sadovska was with her husband simply sitting down on a bench at a park when a cluster bomb exploded and injured both of them. Others in the park were also hit, including two boys playing ping pong. These cluster bombs landed in random places in residential areas and it was often the case that residents at the time of the explosion had prior to it, gathered that much of the danger was dissipating, only to be mistaken when the bombs would all of a sudden explode. One cluster bomb was placed outside of a shop, killing a bystander instantly. He was just waiting outside as his wife was in the store buying pet food. The woman who described the incident to Amnesty International said that she was almost hit in the head with shrapnel that came flying through the window. And that was followed by more explosions. The scene was horrific as many people tried to find cover inside the store. And not far from there, another store where people were standing in line for outreach help, there nearby another bomb exploded, causing mass panic and injuries as shrapnel flew everywhere. Another explosion occurred out the Akademika Pavlova station which injured a number of people standing at the entrance. One person named Ruslan was in his car with two policemen, a 13 year old boy, his brother, and mother when the explosion happened. A man standing outside the car named Sadagad was injured by the explosion. Ruslan, who was also injured by shrapnel, rushed to get Sadagad into the station, from where he would be transferred to a hospital.

A man named Sasha was on his bike just leaving the post office when an explosion occurred and injured him. He was wounded in the arm and chest, but avoided taking shrapnel in the back thanks to an axe he had in his backpack which absorbed the shrapnel and prevented it from entering his body. He credits that for saving his life.

Amnesty International has pointed out that the Ukrainians have also been deploying into civilian areas, and the New York Times reported that Ukrainian forces fired cluster bombs into Russian occupied areas. One example of such was in the village of Husarivka which is in the Kharkiv region. The New York Times reported in an article entitled "To Push Back Russians, Ukrainians Hit a Village With Cluster Munitions" by Thomas Gibbons-Neff and John Ismay, that Ukrainian forces were using cluster bombs to drive the Russians out of the village. In an NYT interview with Yurii Doroshenko, he revealed that a rocket holding cluster munitions landed near his home. It turned out that it was not fired by the Russians, but by the Ukrainian forces, who have been using cluster bombs since October of 2014 during the war in Donbas. Back then, Ukrainian forces as well as Russian forces were cited by human rights organizations for their use of cluster bombs which violated international human rights laws and killed scores of civilians in Donetsk. Shortly after the Russian invasion, Ukrainian forces were still using them on Russian held territory regardless of civilian presence. In that particular strike that Yurii references, no civilians were killed. But throughout the month as Ukrainian forces continued to shell civilian areas, two civilians were confirmed to have been killed by Ukrainian forces as Ukrainian troops tried to recapture the area. The Amnesty International report has largely singled out Russia for the use of cluster bombs. However, the laws of war are applicable to events going back to the war in Donbas, which is when the ICC designated the conflict as an international war between Ukraine and Russia.

Cluster munitions are a combination of "rockets, bombs, missiles, mortar and artillery shells" that break open in mid air and scatter throughout a particular area. Many of the munitions which land there can explode at a later time. The US, Ukraine, and Russia are not signatories to the Convention on Cluster Munitions which banned the use of them starting in 2010. Some in the international human rights community were not surprised to hear that Ukraine as well as Russia was using cluster bombs. However, the international condemnation of Russia's invasion has led some NGOs to turn somewhat of a blind eye to Ukraine's use of banned weapons. And this likely due to a sentiment on their part that largely agrees that Ukraine is justified to do whatever it takes to reclaim their territory, even indirectly endangering and killing their own civilians in the process. Many NGOs that are excusing Ukraine in this case should no longer consider themselves to be in the interest of the civilian population, but only interested in the international political consensus of the moment which upholds that Ukraine has the right to do what ever it takes to reclaim territory unjustifiably captured by Russian forces. At the same time, NGOs must be very careful with such an outlook when entities like Hamas and ISIS are able to argue that their goals are no different than Ukraine's—to essentially drive out an occupying force.

While Ukraine has not denied the use of cluster bombs, they have released a statement following the release of the NYT article saying: *"The Armed Forces of Ukraine strictly adhere to the norms of international humanitarian law. One of our constant priorities is the security of the civilian population. We do not open fire or destroy civilian objects, nor do we use weapons and methods prohibited by the Geneva Conventions."*

The cluster munitions that struck near Yurii's home is reportedly the first time that Ukraine has used cluster munitions during the war post February 24, 2022. The launchpad for the explosives was mounted on a truck a few miles away.

HRW reported that the Russian forces were using cluster bombs since the very start of the invasion. In Kharkiv as shelling continued from both sides of the conflict, Amnesty International documented a case where two cluster munitions launched by Russian forces landed inside of Holy Trinity Church. The munitions had gone through the roof. The church was used for humanitarian outreach and is usually active most of the day. The bombs exploded on the roof and blew shrapnel into the rooms that had been populated just minutes prior to the attack. The Pastor there showed Amnesty International exactly where the damage occurred and how the shrapnel was able to penetrate the walls. Subsequently, pieces of 220mm Uragan rocket which holds 30 cluster munitions were discovered outside in front of the post office. Other parts from the exploding cluster munitions were also found in the area. Moreover, the immediate area surrounding that church had been previously struck by shrapnel from other strikes and explosions. The day after Holy Trinity Church was struck by cluster munitions, it was hit by another rocket strike that landed in the church's courtyard. There were no casualties in that instance.

A Saltivka neighborhood was repeatedly shelled since the start of the Russian invasion. The artillery strikes killed two civilians on April 26th 2022. Among those injured from the blast was Nina Nosonenko and her husband whom were outside of their home when the explosion occurred. Her husband told Amnesty International that the sound leading up to the explosion was not the typical whistling one can hear before a grad rocket strikes. The sound he heard was a crisp sound that lasted shorter before the explosion. He  and his wife, Nina, took cover by running away instead of falling to the ground. He was hit with shrapnel, but after a second explosion, Nina was badly injured. The husband recovered, but Nina remained in the hospital with damaged lungs and an injured back. In the same neighborhood, two elderly women were killed when cluster munitions exploded at a building entrance outside where they sitting with two other people at a bench. After they heard a first explosion occur across the street, they tried to get inside the building. But as they attempted to take cover there, another explosion went off, killing the two older women, and injuring the other two people. One of the women was so badly injured that she had to have her legs amputated.

Seven civilians were killed amid massive shelling and exploding cluster bombs along Heroiv Stalinhrada Ave on April 3rd. On Monyuska Street, two civilians were killed during an explosion that occurred near a bench. A resident from the building near the explosion said she saw the two dead civilians covered in blood, as well as other dead people who just happened to be in the area. She also reported that shrapnel from the explosion had penetrated her home, nearly killing a neighbor who just managed to escape death by moving away from the window just prior to the explosion. Not far from Monyuska Street, another civilian was killed when a cluster bomb exploded. The shrapnel from the blast hit a nearby shop and injured the owner, who had tried to save the life of the man killed by the explosion. This occurred on Fonvizina St where Amnesty International located dozens of craters and pieces of cluster munition along with damage to property. Some of the explosions spanned over 100 ft of street area, leaving a number of craters and dead bodies in its wake. In a suburb area, two civilians were killed inside their homes as explosions blew shrapnel across a series of homes along multiple streets. One person, Oleksandra, reported that her brother was killed after coming out to the garden to rescue her from the explosions. After getting her inside, he was hit by shrapnel which ruptured a main artery in his leg and killed him. Not far from there, Ivan Aiuvszy was killed after shrapnel hit one of his main arteries. Another man will killed by shrapnel while he was visiting the grave of his deceased father. He was with his relatives at the time when the explosion happened. They survived with injuries, but he died as a result of the explosion. His niece, Kateryna, gave an account of the incident to Amnesty International, who found several craters where the explosion happened, along with a number of tombstones damaged by pieces of cluster munition. The Uragan rocket carrying the munitions landed on a farm nearby.

On Amosova Street, dozens of people were killed by artillery strikes conducted by Russian forces between mid March and mid April. The cluster munitions used were comprised of antipersonnel mines which sets off a cascade of explosions. One woman in an apartment reported glass shattering everywhere after hearing an explosion. The room directly above her was struck directly and one of the residents there was killed. She mentioned that damage to the walls left her trapped in her room where the door would not open. The person staying in the first floor apartment room beneath her was killed, and she had just arrived there from the Saltivka residential neighborhood where artillery bombardments were constant. Ironic, considering that her whole purpose for going there was to get away from shelling in her own neighborhood. This would serve to underscore just how perilous things were for residents in Kharkiv. One of the residents of the apartment building reported a number of civilian deaths in the apartment building without disclosing their names. His tragedy was only hours after an explosion at a playground which injured five people. The worst injury in that case required a foot amputation.

Amnesty International was able to narrow down exactly which type of rocket was fired into civilian areas. Upon investgation at multiple sites in Kharkiv, they were able to conclude that the weapon launched was 220mm Uragan rocket containing 30 individual munitions, each containing steel pellets. These rockets are unguided and after they are launched, they release the submunitions while in flight, dispersing them over an area as extensive as 100 square meters. Many of the munitions don't explode on impact, but can do so at a later time which essentially turns them into land mines. The scale of damage this type of weapon causes is why the international community moved to ban them in 2008 at the Convention of Cluster Munitions.

On March 1st 2022, Russian forces fired rockets that landed on Nova Bavariya Avenue, killing seven residents that lived in the residential building just opposite a crane factory which was also struck. There were pieces of Uragan rockets left from the explosion. Kostiantyn Neshcheret lost his mother, brother, and friend, all of whom were near the front of the building when the rocket hit. He had gone to the store and that was when the blast took place. Others who were killed like Iryna Lisovska, Yurii Shesterov, and Stanislay Bacanov all died inside their apartment. Roma Demianenko was killed as he stood outside the building and was "blown to pieces" as one person described it. Meanwhile, the hospitals were inundated with wounded patients from the blast, many of whom were hit while waiting in line for humanitarian assistance. Residents described the horror of living through the conflict and the aspect of dealing with not knowing which day you will live or die. One person described the situation in Kharkiv to be akin to a game of Russian Roulette. In many cases, people are going about their daily program and then all of a sudden were being maimed or killed by unexpected rocket fire. Some people were sheltering in the basement and upon going up just for a minute, a blast would hit the area. One person, a 59 year old woman named Tetiana Oleksandrivna, on March 13th had only left her basement for a minute before she was struck by shrapnel from an explosion. Her neighbor had only gone out to smoke before he was killed by the strike. In Kharkiv, there was no way to apprehend when danger would manifest. A 60 year old man was sweeping the floor in the hallway entrance to his building before he was struck and killed by a rocket. On April 23rd, Oleksandr Marchenko suffered multiple wounds trying to get into a building to escape a number of explosion nearby on Heroiv Pratsi Street. As soon as he made it to the entrance, he was hit by shrapnel in his stomach and back, which punctured his lungs and liver. Several others in the area that day were killed by the explosions.

One woman named Veronika had to have her right leg removed after an unguided rocket hit a playground near her house in the Saltinkva residential area on March 12th 2022. Several people were killed and injured, according to Amnesty International. Veronika was on a bench when it happened and recalled hearing that all too familiar whistling sound that occurs before a rocket strikes its target. All she remembers after that is being in the hospital without her right leg. She often suffers phantom leg syndrome, where she would feel an urge to scratch her foot that is no longer there. The suffering endured by civilians during war should make everyone rethink their support of any country's military objective. In modern warfare, the civilian costs is enormous and in many cases, those civilian components of a nation would just prefer for hostilities to end, no matter the political costs. When people get caught up in the geopolitics, it becomes easy to forget about other aspects that are very much part of the conflict. There have been numerous foreigners go to Ukraine to fight, only to leave shortly thereafter upon seeing firsthand the devastation of an artillery strike. And in Kharkiv, the devastation seemed endless. A 63 year old woman was hit by shrapnel as she stood outside of a grocery store on February 28th. The store was not far from where she lived on Klochkivska Street, and she was standing in line outside the store at the time of blast. Just before the rocket hit, other people in line took cover and ran away from the area. However, she told Amnesty International that she was paralyzed by fear and ultimately lost her leg as a result of the explosion. Another man on Amosova Street, 63 years old man named Yurii, lost both feet when a rocket struck his apartment building while he was inside laying on his sofa. This occurred on April 30th.

On March 3rd, Hanna Lakhno, Konstiantyn Lymar, and Andrii Ihasimo were all killed by artillery bombardments in the Saltivka neighbourhood. All three were friends. Hanna and Konstiantyn were preparing to leave the city; they had their belongings packed and were ready to evacuate. But shortly after, as they were standing outside of the building where they lived, along with their friend Andrii, they were struck by rocket fire which obliterated them. Konstiantyn was blown into pieces, and the other suffered a gruesome outcome as well, all of which made it hard for their bodies to be properly identified. Not far from the tragedy on the same day, another area in the neighborhood which had previously been struck by shelling, leading to the death of a civilian, encountered another strike. A 62 year old man was injured in the strike as he was inside his apartment. He related to Amnesty that three shells penetrated his apartment. The injuries he suffered led to his arm being amputated. Another person who lived on the same street(Buchmy in the Saltivka neighborhood) reported seeing four residents killed by shelling near building 36 as the paramedics were trying to provide aid to those injured in the blast. Throughout much of the shelling, residents had only a small window of opportunity to evade the strikes, but in many cases they could not know from where or which direction the shelling would be coming from. In many instances, people could hear a whistling sound followed by a blast. On March 3rd, there were two people who were killed while trying to get to safety in their car. This was a mother and son. The son was trying to get his mother out of the area, but both ended up being killed by the shelling. The tragedy of civilian deaths is even more pronounced when in many cases the victims were maimed, killed, and obliterated right in front of their loved ones. In other cases, death would occur in the most inconspicuous circumstances. One man named Yurii, 60 years old, was killed by shrapnel from an explosion on Heroiv Street just as he was asking two people sitting in front of a building entrance for a cigarette. It has all too often been the case in Ukraine, that many of the victims were not anticipating death at the time it happened. In one such case as the Saltivka neighborhood continued to be shelled relentlessly, two people recalled being hurt by rocket fire on a day that they did not expect any shelling. In fact, prior to the strike, as one of the residents recalled, it was quiet with no indication that danger was imminent. And then all of a sudden an explosion from outside shattered the window. The woman who lived there was wounded in the leg by shrapnel as her and her husband were trying to evacuate the apartment and get to the basement. As we see in these incidents documented by Amnesty International that the level of carnage cannot be understated. In many instances, an entire family would be in their homes as one of the family members there would be killed by a shell as they inhabited a different room in the house. This was what happened in the Tkachov household. The father Serhii Tkachov was killed in a strike on his home as other members of the family survived due to being in a different part of the house at the time of the blast. The wife was in the bedroom, the son was in his bedroom, while the father, Serhii, was in the kitchen where the blast occurred. It caused the ceiling to collapse on top of him, trapping him as fire engulfed him. His family witnessed this.

In a suburb situated near the edges of Kharkiv where Ukrainian forces were blocking the Russians from entering the city, shelling killed a man named Konstiantyn inside the entrance to a house. In another example of shelling on March 16th, the victims did not hear the typical whistling sound that indicates a rocket will blast nearby. Another man named Konstiantyn was sitting in front of his home with four others when shelling hit an area just a few feet away from his house. The shrapnel blew into his chest and killed him as he bled to death.

Amnesty International in their Kharkiv report documented that Ukrainian forces were deploying their troops and equipment into residential areas, which confirms other reports ascertaining similar allegations. Amnesty also mentioned that Ukrainian forces were using such tactics that endangered civilian lives. According to the Amnesty International report "ANYONE CAN DIE AT ANY TIME:  Indiscriminate attacks by Russian forces in Kharkiv, Ukraine", it was reported to them that Ukrainian forces were launching strikes from the Industrialnyi, Shevchenkivskyi and Saltivka districts. Civilian casualties were rampant in the Saltivka neighborhoods as documented by Amnesty. However, in main body of their report which described specific incidents of casualties in the Saltivka district, Amnesty did not mention or document cases where Ukrainian forces were firing nearby and thus triggering Russian artillery back into the civilian areas. The only documented cases in the report of Ukrainian forces deploying into residential neighborhoods was in a note near the end of the report. Amnesty International was present in the Saltivka neighborhood when they heard "outgoing fire" on April 26th. Residents on Buchmy street, according to the report, said that shelling started on February 25th when Ukrainian forces *"deployed a Howitzer on the street opposite Building 36, roughly 120 metres from it."* One resident from the Saltivka neighborhood told Amnesty International that *"After two or three hours of this Howitzer beginning to shoot, we received opposite fire from the Russian side,"*

And according to the Amnesty International report:

*"he added that the howitzer was first located on the street in front of a garage shop, and was then moved to the nearby courtyard behind the garage, and after three days it was moved out of the area but Russian forces continued shelling for several weeks. Amnesty International delegates inspected the site, finding vehicle tracks consistent with military activity, as well as a large crater from a strike right next to where the resident said the Howitzer was parked. The site was guarded by a man who said he was a former soldier, and who restricted access to the area. In Pokotylivka, a suburb southwest of Kharkiv, Ukrainian Territorial Defense Forces used some small outbuildings in the yard of the compound of a medical laboratory as a base. The compound is surrounded by residential buildings and is located opposite a school which serves as a humanitarian hub. The laboratory was bombed by Russian forces – an apparent air strike -- on the morning of 28 April. Although the medical laboratory was mostly empty, as most employees worked remotely, two employees who were present were injured. In addition, two members of the Territorial Defense Forces were killed and six injured. At the site, near the outbuildings in the compound, Amnesty International researchers found several empty munitions boxes, some of which had labels indicating that they had contained KPOM-2 scatterable mine canisters."*

Amnesty International did not mention Ukraine's use of cluster munitions, but did ask them to refrain from using them. In April of 2022, Russia has removed the registration of Amnesty International, Human Rights Watch, as well as other non-profit organizations over western bias. However, Russia should reconsider re-instating Amnesty International's Moscow office since while Amnesty has been caught up in the western sentiments regarding the perception of the war being unjustified, Amnesty has still, nonetheless, shown that they will document all evidence regardless of which side it implicates, even though at times Amnesty may still only convey a greater condemnation towards one side of the conflict. There willingness to at least adhere to fair documentation should be seen as something conducive to a satisfactory outcome for both sides of the conflict. Delays in applying scrutiny to both sides of a military conflict only serves to imperil civilians, leaving them at the mercy of the armed forces perceived to be within their right to take action. This was the case for the US military during their initial invasion of Afghanistan. Immediately following the 9/11 tragedy in 2001, the wave of outcry demanding justice for the victims of 9/11 had a pervasive impact on a global scale, but ultimately, in retrospect, put Afghan civilians at the complete mercy of US military objectives which at that time could not be questioned by any entity without them being seen as siding with terrorists. Had a hard-line neutral observer remained astute from the outset of the war, scores of lives may have been saved. But all too often, the horror of civilian death is only recognized in hindsight when it is too late.

On July 3rd, 2022, Ukrainian forces fired 3 Tochka-U missiles into the Russian city of Belgorod, causing 4 civilian deaths in a residential area. The missiles were shot down by Russia's air-defense systems, but the smash-up caused fragments of rocket debris to fall onto and destroy the homes and residential areas just below. This is the first time since the conflict began, that Russia has suffered civilian casualties from the war. Ukraine denied responsibility but said that it was karma because of all the civilian deaths in Ukraine caused by Russian forces. Ukraine's Interior Ministry believed that Russia orchestrated the attack in order to justify its military purposes. Eleven apartment buildings and 39 homes were destroyed. The victims included a family from Kharkiv who had migrated to Belgorod in order to escape the fighting. Western media downplayed the incident, while Russia insisted that the strike deliberately targeted the civilian population in Belgorod. This comes on the heels of the Russian missile strike in Kremenchuk, which destroyed a factory believed to have been used for military purposes, as well as a nearby mall where civilians were killed. Both incidents mark a point of dangerous escalation in the conflict, where both sides may seek revenge on the other by targeting outright, any civilian infrastructure. Since Russia had dismissed all of its western-based human rights investigators, the west would have no way of assessing the scope of civilian casualties caused by Ukrainian forces. This leads to both sides pushing a one-sided narrative that justifies protracting the conflict. In order to avoid this, Russia may need to reinstate Amnesty International, which is perhaps the only human rights organization that has proven, despite their western lean and anti-Russian outlook, to be willing to document infractions by both sides of the conflict.

## Chapter 10: Mercenaries in Ukraine

Russian continued to warn the west about supplying Ukraine with heavy weapons. Much of the weapons aid to Ukraine from western countries started back in 2014, when it was mostly non-lethal weapons being sent. The US however didn't start supplying high tech weapons to Ukraine until 2018, sending Javelin anti-tank missiles. Turkey also sold some of their drones to Ukraine in 2019. Much of the supply sent to Ukraine was instrumental in Ukraine's defense against Russian forces in the western part of the country. The influx of weapons steadily increased in the months leading up to the Russian invasion when countries like the UK decided to supply Ukraine with anti-tank weapons. Germany, however, didn't really get around to supplying Ukraine with heavy weapons until some time later after the Russian invasion. While western countries have individually supplied Ukraine with military aid, NATO as a military bloc has refrained from sending weapons to Ukraine. The most critical piece of aid which could have allowed Ukraine a more adequate defensive operation would have been fighter jets, but the west refused to provide such, fearing escalation. Russia had begun threatening to use its nuclear capability against western nations if the west tried to provide fighter jets to Ukraine. There was some speculation that the west would nonetheless attempt to get f-35 fighter jets into Ukraine, but after some miscommunication, such arrangements never fell thru. At one point the US confirmed they were prepared to supply the jets, but within 24 hours walked back the announced and denied they would be providing Ukraine with the f-35s. NATO also refused to send troops into Ukraine to help them fend off the Russian invasion. However, there was no shortage of anti-tank weapons supplied to Ukraine. 20000 of them were sent to Ukraine following Russia's invasion. Both the EU and the US sent billions of dollars in aid to the country to help bolster their military and protection protocols for the civilian population. By April, the total number of anti-aircraft and anti-tank weapons totaled 25000 and 60000 respectively. By May, Ukraine had altogether received 12 billion dollars worth of aid from western countries. This was followed by another pledge from the US to provide 40 billion dollars worth of military aid.

Both Russia and Ukraine has been aided by the presence of foreign troops. Western media companies such as Reuters would refer to Russia's middle east volunteer fighters as mercenaries, while Russia would use similar terminology to describe Ukraine's volunteer fighters from the UK and the US. The breakaway regions in Georgia sent troops to Ukraine to help Russia. For Ukraine, many of the foreign fighters had come from other parts of Europe, and the Ukrainian government offered to drop visa requirements for anyone coming from abroad to fight with the Ukrainian military. Zelenskyy formed the International Legion of Territorial Defense of Ukraine and relegated it for foreign troops. Altogether 20,000 foreign nationals from 52 countries ended up in Ukraine fighting against the Russian forces. Nearly 66,000 Ukrainian that were living outside of the country returned to help Ukraine fight the war. The US, meanwhile, provided critical intelligence assessments on Russian troop location which allowed Ukraine to sink Russian ships and kill Russian generals.

When it came to the topic of foreign fighters a clear double standard was applied, which ultimately backfired when volunteer soldiers from the UK and the US had ended up being captured by DPR and Russian forces. Despite repeatedly calling Putin's volunteer fighters "mercenaries", the US and UK media companies and government officials insisted that the those British and American fighters fighting with Ukrainian forces on behalf of Ukraine were volunteers and not mercenaries. Situations like this is when the media has to be careful of the policy they set for others, because it will decide one's ability to persuade all parties of one's own status. The double standards applied only serve to imperil more lives in the war. At this point going forward all volunteer fighters, both on the Ukrainian side and Russian side have to be considered volunteer fighters protected under the Geneva Convention.

Two British and a Moroccan fighting in Ukraine alongside Ukrainian forces were captured by DPR forces and later sentenced to death. Following the sentence, both the UK and the United Nations insisted that the captured fighters were not mercenaries, but prisoners of war protected under the Geneva Convention. This comes after western media repeatedly calling Russia's volunteer fighters, "mercenaries", making the UN and other western organizations seem hypocritical. Ukraine's foreign ministry also stated that all foreign fighters fighting for Ukraine should be protected under the Geneva Convention and be regarded as POWs, not mercenaries.

During the war in Iraq, volunteer fighters were repeatedly referred to as "mercenaries" by US forces. Now in Ukraine, US officials are working tirelessly to guarantee POW status for two American fighters detained by Russian forces. Both American volunteer fighters were captured by Russian troops after being left stranded by their unit. They had been fighting in Kharkiv. Both were US military veterans. Alexander Drueke, formerly US Army, did two tours in Iraq. The other American fighter captured, Andy Huynh, was a former US Marine. Both were operating in Ukraine and taking orders from the SBU, Ukraine's Security Service, and were told to provide cover so Ukrainian forces could retreat. Upon retreat the Ukrainian forces were being followed by Russia tanks. Meanwhile, Huynh had been at an outpost with an RPG getting ready to fire upon the Russian tanks after it open fired on the retreating Ukrainian soldiers. When Huynh did fire his Rocket-Propelled Grenade, it missed. After the Ukrainian forces had left the area, leaving Huynh and Drueke stranded in the woods, the American fighters eventually stumbled into a village nearby, and that is when they were confronted by Russian troops and had no choice but to surrender. American officials insisted that the soldiers were not mercenaries, but prisoners of war. But Russian officials have already concluded that they were mercenaries fighting as "soldiers of fortune." When the two American fighters were interviewed by RT, they warned other Americans who were thinking about coming to fight for Ukraine to reconsider. They also said that they were being treated humanely by their Russian captors, but were aware that they could face the death penalty. During the RT interview, both Americans admitted to have been swayed by the western narrative of the war, and ultimately ended up disappointed with the lack of preparation and corruption within Ukraine's "International Legion." The testimony is very similar to other foreign fighters that managed to escape Ukraine and make it back to their home country. Subsequently, after leaving Ukraine's international legion, the American volunteer fighters both sought to join a more tactical unit. This when they discovered the 'Task Force Baguette' in eastern Ukraine, a unit comprised mostly of American and French veterans. Russia considers the unit to be a foreign mercenary group. While US officials are working hard to secure their release, the US state department continued to urge American not to go to Ukraine.

After Russia invaded Ukraine, Zelenskyy, like President Putin, announced that his country was accepting volunteer fighters. Subsequently, with the aid of western media, many citizens in the western world were compelled to join the fighting. There are also foreign fighters in Ukraine that are organizing outside of the command of the Ukrainian army. However, those Americans joining the fight in Ukraine are in danger of not only being considered mercenaries if they are captured by the enemy, but are also in danger of violating the Neutrality Act if they join Ukraine's forces within US territory or organize a militant group against Russia within the US. The law also forbids Americans from fighting against a country that is at peace with the United States. Currently Russia is at peace with the US, so according to the Neutrality Act, Americans, when they are within the United States, joining the military of another country or forming their own private groups to fight against a country that the US is not at war with is a violation.

The Neutrality Act states in 18 U.S. Code § 958:
*Any citizen of the United States who, within the jurisdiction thereof, accepts and exercises a commission to serve a foreign prince, state, colony, district, or people, in war, against any prince, state, colony, district, or people, with whom the United States is at peace, shall be fined under this title or imprisoned not more than three years, or both.*

The Neutrality Act states in 18 U.S.C. 959:
*(a)Whoever, within the United States, enlists or enters himself, or hires or retains another to enlist or enter himself, or to go beyond the jurisdiction of the United States with intent to be enlisted or entered in the service of any foreign prince, state, colony, district, or people as a soldier or as a marine or seaman on board any vessel of war, letter of marque, or privateer, shall be fined under this title or imprisoned not more than three years, or both.*
*(b)This section shall not apply to citizens or subjects of any country engaged in war with a country with which the United States is at war, unless such citizen or subject of such foreign*

*country shall hire or solicit a citizen of the United States to enlist or go beyond the jurisdiction of the United States with intent to enlist or enter the service of a foreign country. Enlistments under this subsection shall be under regulations prescribed by the Secretary of the Army.*
*(c)This section and sections 960 and 961 of this title shall not apply to any subject or citizen of any foreign prince, state, colony, district, or people who is transiently within the United States and enlists or enters himself on board any vessel of war, letter of marque, or privateer, which at the time of its arrival within the United States was fitted and equipped as such, or hires or retains another subject or citizen of the same foreign prince, state, colony, district, or people who is transiently within the United States to enlist or enter himself to serve such foreign prince, state, colony, district, or people on board such vessel of war, letter of marque, or privateer, if the United States shall then be at peace with such foreign prince, state, colony, district, or people.*

The Neutrality Act states in 18 U.S. Code § 960:
*Whoever, within the United States, knowingly begins or sets on foot or provides or prepares a means for or furnishes the money for, or takes part in, any military or naval expedition or enterprise to be carried on from thence against the territory or dominion of any foreign prince or state, or of any colony, district, or people with whom the United States is at peace, shall be fined under this title or imprisoned not more than three years, or both.*

The reason for the Neutrality Act was to protect America from being drawn into a war as a result of actions taken by American citizens against a nation that the US is not at war with. The American fighters captured seemed to have joined fight in Ukraine from Ukrainian territory, which would not be in violation of the Neutrality Act. The Neutrality Act forbids Americans on American soil from privately organizing against a nation that the US is not at war with. It also prohibits anyone in US territory from planning, intending, of saving money to go to go to another country to fight against a nation that the US is not at war with.

A danger posed by Americans going to Ukraine to fight is that it can easily be construed by Russian officials as something that is condoned and authorized by the US government, a perception that could escalate and broaden the conflict. The US has repeatedly stated to the American public that Americans should not be going to Ukraine to fight.

A number of foreign volunteer fighters that went to Ukraine to join the foreign legion reported a serious lack of preparation on the part of unit commanders. Many of the volunteers were given no training, no weapons and still placed in dangerous situations. It was also observed that many volunteer fighters who had previously served in the US military during the wars in Iraq and Afghanistan were completely frightened and unprepared for combat involving an advanced Russian military. Many of them were compelled to flee Ukraine after seeing that fighting the Russian army was vastly different from fighting against insurgents in the middle east who had no air force and no advanced weaponry. In many cases, the fighting in Ukraine involved little to no contact with Russian military personnel, and it was often the case that fighters spent most of their time cooped up in trenches taking refuge from constant artillery bombardments. A Belgium newspaper called Het Laatste Nieuws said over half of the foreign fighters that went to Ukraine already left the country after initially feeling called to go and fight. Many who fought with NATO and US forces were not use to fighting without air support and medics, two of which were absent for many units fighting in Ukraine. Moreover, a major fear concerning foreign fighters in Ukraine is that Russia could, in the event of capturing American fighters, accuse the US of deploying them to Ukraine, which could ignite a serious escalation that both the US and NATO has been trying to avoid since February 24, 2022 when Russia launched a full-scale assault on the country. Meanwhile, Ukrainian forces had become concerned about the strain that under-trained foreign fighters are placing on military operations. Because many of the foreign fighters are unable to speak the Ukrainian language, they are thus forces to stay alongside someone who can speak their native language, which in turn makes them inflexible in terms of how the Ukrainian military could make use of them.

## Chapter 11: Russian Assault on Sievierodonetsk

When it comes to casualties, both the Russian side and the Ukrainian side are believed to have misconstrued the numbers for the sake of keeping troop morale elevated. The BBC reported that Ukraine factored in injured Russian troops into the total number of Russian soldiers killed in the conflict. Many of the official conflict record keepers have not been able to substantiate the claims made by both sides. Both the UN and the Office of the United Nations High Commissioner for Human Rights(OHCHR) are at odds about the number of civilian casulties. OHCHR believes the figure is higher than the one the UN is reporting.

As of mid-June, a critical battle waged on in Sievierodonetsk in the Donbas region of eastern Ukraine. While Sievierodonetsk is located in the Luhansk Oblast, one of the breakaway regions, the city of Sievierodonetsk remained part of Ukraine. However in June, the Russian forces began to surround the city. Both Sievierodonetsk and Lysychansk hosted many serious clashes between Ukrainian forces and Separatist forces during the war in Donbas back in 2014. Shortly after Russian forces invaded Ukraine in February of 2022, Russian troops immediately began shelling Sievierodonetsk and clashes between Russian and Ukrainian forces erupted all over the city. Ukrainian troops initially repelled the Russian forces from entering Sievierodonetsk. In the meantime, however, Russian forces managed to gain control over much of the surrounding region in Luhansk, capturing Rubizhne and Popasna, two cities very close to Sievierodonetsk. The Russian troops continued to shell Sievierodonetsk as the Ukrainian continued to resist the Russian advance. Meanwhile, many civilians in the city began to flee, and in April, Russian troops began moving into vacant areas of the Donbas region. Ukrainian forces began suffering massive casualties as a result of intense fighting, losing around 100 troops a day and imploring western nations to provide more heavy weapons. In early May, both the Russian troops and LPR fighters began securing areas just outside of Sievierodonetsk. The strategy was to take control over all the nearby villages and effectively surround the city and cut off its access to the outside. The Ukrainian holdout, nonetheless, refused to surrender, despite ultimatums from LPR and Russian fighters. Russian forces continued to attack villages surrounding Sievierodonetsk—Rubizhne, Voevodivka, Popasna and Bilohorivka encountered significant Russian fighting, and before long, Russian forces encircled the city. They were then in position to bombard it relentlessly after the LPR defeated the Ukrainian forces in the battle of Rubizhne. Russia subsequently halted the ground advance and strictly resorted to artillery strikes on both Sievierodonetsk and Lysychansk. While the Russian forces were largely staved off in the north, they were able to make gains south of the city. In late May, Russian forces began a ground assault and tried to make their way further into Sievierodontsk and break off into multiple pockets within the city. In the west, the supply lines were being destroyed by Russian artillery. The Russian troops made minor advances on May 28th, but by this time both sides of the conflict were suffering heavy casualties. Russia did not want to overextend its commitment to add reinforcements to the region, and at this time reinforcing LPR fighters was proving to be very difficult. The next day, fighting erupted in the middle of Sievierodonetsk as some Russian troops were able to breach Ukrainian resistance at the outskirts. Shortly thereafter, Russia gained control over 80% of the city, causing many Ukrainian troops to retreat and prepare for a counteroffensive. At the start of June, Russian artillery struck a nitric acid tank at the Azot chemical plant, where roughly 800 civilians had been hiding in bomb shelters underneath. Despite the Russian advance into the city centre, Ukrainian troops managed to kill 200 Russian soldiers and regain some of the lost territory in Sievierodonetsk after launching a counter offensive on June 3rd. Many of Ukraine's foreign fighters were also active in the city. Despite the newfound momentum, Russia had cut off supply lines, blowing up bridges that lead into the city, making it difficult for Ukrainian troops to access deliveries of food and medicine into Sievierodonetsk. The Ukrainian Ministry of Defense accused Russia of putting its non-Russian military personnel in danger for the sake of minimizing casualties within the Russian army. The governor of Luhansk, Serhiy Haidai, was confounded by the sheer size of the Russian military arsenal in terms of troops and equipment. President Zelenskyy repeated the same sentiments, despite vowing that Ukrainian troops will continue resisting. Yet no one was certain as to who was controlling what, in and around the city, but Ukrainian officials continued to remain steadfast, ensuring everyone that Ukrainian forces would continue to hold out. This was amid Russian reports that Ukrainian forces were depleted of critical supplies and troops. A short while later, the Luhansk governor would admit that Ukrainian forces had been pushed back as a result of Russian shelling, leaving 800 civilians trapped in the Azot chemical factory. By June 9th, the Russian forces would have control over 90% of the city. Ukrainian forces attempted to lure Russian forces into an urban combat scenario, but the lack of influx of weapons and other equipment left Ukrainian forces stagnant. The urban fighting continued and casualties continued to mount on both sides, but Ukrainian officials were admitting that they were taking heavy losses and that Russia was in control over much of Sievierodonetsk. Ukrainian officials also continued to reiterate that the Russians had a significant advantage of manpower and artillery. However, the LPR officials accused Ukraine of launching strikes from the Azot plant, potentially using the civilians there as human shields. On June 13th , the last remaining bridges attaching Sievierodonetsk to other parts of Luhansk had been destroyed by Russian forces and left Ukrainian forces indefinitely stranded inside the city with no supply lines or escape routes. Up to this point, the carnage and death in Sievierodonetsk had become so significant that Ukrainian officials stopped counting casualties. But much like other parts of Ukraine, there were reports of Russian shelling of soft targets like schools and churches, as well as humanitarian centers. The mayor as of late May said that roughly 1500 civilians were killed in Sievierodonetsk since the beginning of the Russian invasion on February 24, 2022. On June 25, 2022, the Russian forces took full control of Sievierodonetsk, forcing Ukrainian forces to retreat and seek higher ground in Lysychansk in a move which allows Ukraine to prepare for a future counter-assault. This was the largest setback for Ukrainian forces. However, Ukrainian officials insist that the withdrawal was strictly tactical, and that the newly arrived HIMARS rocket systems will allow Ukraine to strike targets in Russian-occupied areas of the country, making it possible for Ukrainian forces to recapture lost territories. But unfortunately within a few days, Lysychansk would fall to the Russians.

## Chapter 12: POWs and Refugees

When it comes to POW count, the numbers have been difficult to verify. Ukraine's ambassador reported that a platoon from the 74th Guards Motor Rifle Brigade operating in Kemerovo surrendered to Ukrainian forces early in the war and said that they were not aware of orders to kill Ukrainian soldiers. Russia says that they have 572 Ukrainian soldiers in custody as of March 2nd, 2022. while Ukraine has reported having 562 Russian soldiers held captive. This was as of March 20th. The first prisoner exchange was conducted and involved 10 Russian POWs being exchanged for five Ukrainian POWs along with the mayor of Melitopol, whom was in Russian custody. In late March, 21 Russian POWs comprising of soldiers and sailors were exchanged for 29 Ukrainian POWs consisting of soldiers and sailors. At the beginning of April, more Ukrainian POWs were exchanged in a prisoner swap for an unverified number of Russian troops. Both Ukraine and Russia were urged by international human rights organizations to stay in compliance with international law concerning the treatment of prisoners. Ukrainian troops were posting videos on social media in which they were humiliating Russian troops in their custody. One video showed a Ukrainian soldier shooting Russian POWs in the knees, while another uploaded to Telegram showed a Ukrainian soldier executing a Russian prisoner. Ukraine has subsequently launched an investigation into the incident. Russian troops were also posting videos which showed that Russian soldiers were humiliating Ukrainian POWs, forcing them to sing songs of a pro-Russian theme. Many of the Ukrainian POWs shown in the videos had bruises, which evoked concern from UN human rights monitors.

Since February 24, 2022 when the Russian invasion began, eastern Europe has had to face the greatest European refugee crisis since the Yugoslav war in 1999. However, preparations for this was made in advance of the war when Ukraine estimated the amount of evacuations that would have to be conducted. Many of the surrounding nations had plans in place to deal with mass displacement of Ukrainians. Just in the first seven days after the start of the invasion, a million Ukrainians fled the country. The number would rise significantly higher as the war went on. By late May, the number of evacuees was estimated to be close to seven million. The vast majority of these were women, children, and the elderly. Men in Ukraine at the time of the invasion were not allowed to leave the country. This went for not only ethnic Ukrainian men between 18 and 60, but also for non-Ukrainian men living in the country. If a man was either a single father, supporting more than three children, or supporting children that were disabled, then he was allowed to evacuate the country. Despite the restrictions, many men in Ukraine chose to fight regardless. Altogether within Ukraine, the remaining Ukrainian residents displaced were roughly in the range of 8 million. The UN High Commission for Refugees tallied the number of refugees from Ukraine situated in neighboring countries as a result of the war. This was as of May 13th. In Poland, there were a little over 3 million Ukrainian refugees there. In Romania, 901,696. In Hungary, Moldova, and Slovakia, there were close to 500,000 Ukrainian refugees in each of those countries. Belarus took in about 27000 Ukrainian refugees, while Russia had taken in around 800,000. As of late March, over 300,000 were in the Czech Republic, and around 80,000 evacuated to Turkey by April. Ukrainian exodus from Ukraine was followed by the EU invoking the Temporary Protection Directive, which would give Ukrainians a temporary citizenship in the EU country they are taking refuge in, in which they would be able to secure housing and employment.

Ukraine fears that refugees evacuated from Ukraine to Russia might be sent to camps in separatist regions or within Russia. Russian had evacuated around 121000 Mariupol residents, and Ukraine is concerned that many of them will end up in prison camps and forced into slave labor meant for helping develop new cities. Ukrainian security officials reported that Russia is planning to build a concentration camp for Ukrainian refugees. Many evacuees that had lived in the southeastern parts of Ukraine that were not hit by military activity have expressed a desire to return.

Russia since the invasion in February of 2022 has experienced an outflow of people seeking refuge from political constraints implemented by the Russian government. The fear of Russia's crackdown on dissidence has caused 300,000 people living in Russia to flee in what has been the biggest exodus of Russians from Russia since 1917 when the Bolshevik Revolution was taking place. Many of them were highly skilled workers critical to the Russian economy, and a few of them tried to go to Ukraine to help

Ukrainians fight the war, despite themselves being Russian. By May, it had been reported that nearly four million Russians vacated since the beginning of the invasion.

Ukraine, known as the bread basket, of Europe is one of the biggest exporters of grain. They account for nearly 9% of the world's wheat. But wheat is not the only commodity that Ukraine exports. They also export maize, barley, and rapeseed, accounting for 13% of the world's supply for each. Ukraine is a massive exporter sunflower oil as well. But the Russian invasion has led to food shortages, especially in countries that rely on Ukraine's exports. Right before the war began, 6 million tons of wheat were all set up to exported from Ukraine—this along with 15 million tons of corn. However, the war would prevent those food supplies from leaving Ukraine, thereby disrupting a very sensitive supply chain, which would lead to a ripple effect of food shortages. Russia, a major exporter of fertilizer and other components critical to soil health, was also blocked from exporting much of its goods due to sanctions applied against them. The book "The Fall of the US Dollar: A Second Coming of the Non-Aggression Pact" argues that sanctions levied upon Russia will only work in Russia's favor and only cause the Russian ruble to grow in value:

*Due to Russia's invasion of Ukraine in February of 2022, worldwide sanctions have been imposed on Russia. These have caused inflation in Russia to rise to nearly 10%, and many analyst are forecasting it will surpass 20% by the end of March 2022 as the Russian currency, the Ruble, continues to collapse. Russia relies on imported goods such as cars, household appliances, televisions and smartphones, but multiple sanctions levied by the west against Russia has effectuated massive price increases among those products. The price of new cars rose 15%. Russia is also worried about how a reliance on imports for its agricultural industry, such as potato seeds will affect the economic situation. In response to the rising inflation and as a measure to stabilize prices, Russia's Central Bank has raised interest rates to 20%. According to the BBC, the sanctions applied against Russia for invading Ukraine in 2022 are as follows: The United States banned its oil and gas imports from Russia. The UK said they would gradually phase out their Russian oil imports by 2030. And Germany and the EU pledged to reduce their reliance* on Russian oil by seeking alternative sources of energy before 2030. The west has also frozen Russia's foreign holdings of dollars and euros, and restricted banks from doing business with Russia's central bank. Some of Russia's banks are being restricted from the SWIFT banking system, which will prevent them from conducting international transactions. This would also delay any accounts receivable owed to Russia for its oil and gas exports. The UK has frozen the assets of all Russian banks, and restricted their access to the UK financial system. The result is that Russia would not be able to raise funds or borrow money within the UK. A number of goods have been restricted from being sent to Russia, while the UK, US, EU, and Canada have banned Russian airlines from its airspace. Assets belonging to Russian president Vladimir Putin has been frozen as well. Russia in response has banned much of their exports to the west, exports which consist of various products, such as telecoms, medical, vehicle, agricultural, electrical equipment and timber. Russia has also stopped making interest payments to foreign investors holding Russian government bonds, and they also squeezed the liquidity of stocks and bonds held by foreign investors. In light of these developments, one can see how the sanctions will have a detrimental impact on western Europe. Not only in terms of acquiring adequate energy supplies, which might no longer be provided by Russia, but also in terms of food production. Russia and Ukraine account for a third of the world's wheat/grain and barley exports, but now with these sanctions levied upon Russia by the west, along with Russia retaliating by stopping its wheat/grain  and fertilizer exports, much of the world that is dependent on such food supplies will have to face the prospect of significant food shortages, and at the same time deal with the impact of how fertilizer shortages will disrupt the very sensitive farming protocols, which could keep crop yields very low. Places like Egypt, Tunisia, and Lebanon are dependent on grain/wheat imported from Russia. Everything considered, Ukraine and Russia are basically world powers in the global food supply industry.

These sanctions against Russia present a catch 22. In one sense, Russia is cut off from the financial sector in the west, but at the same time, they will be able to accrue a surplus inventory from oil and grain production. This leaves the likelihood that

*Russia will become a major player in ethanol production, as many industries around the world are seeking to transition from 100% petroleum to using a mix of petroleum and biofuels, before eventually going 100% biofuel. With wheat shortages in the west and the middle east, Russia would be able to become the major player in ethanol production since ethanol is produced from wheat and corn, which would be in surplus amounts in Russia as a result of halting their export. This prospect could coincide with a spectacular Ruble recovery, should Russia decide to sell ethanol in exchange for rubles and at the same time undercut US corn production by refusing to export nitrogen fertilizer. This would in effect stifle US ethanol production because without adequate fertilizer, the west would not have the surplus corn to produce greater amounts of ethanol. In this scenario, much of the corn would have to be designated for human consumption. As a result of the competition being eroded in the ethanol market, the rising Ruble would not undermine the competitive viability of Russia's export of ethanol fuels, should those fuels be sold for Rubles. The extra wheat and corn could also be used as a bargaining chip in places like the middle east and Africa, whom will insist on resuming grain imports from Russia. In this manner, Russia could seek out ospolitik-type agreements in which Russia would attempt to normalize relations with other nations by being granted some media influence in exchange for grain shipments or fertilizer. This would be for the sake of controlling how Russia is viewed as a nation within other countries. This would also give Russia more influence in the middle east in terms of being able to mediate peace between warring nations, despite Russia belonging to a consortium of Shiite nations like Syria, and Iran. A growing dependency on Russia's production of oil, gas, and ethanol blends would bring the west back into Russia's sphere of influence, should urgency about carbon emissions continue to grow worldwide. This would also coincide with a greater global demand for Rubles, which would allow Russia to stimulate their economy by safely increasing the amount of rubles circulating within their financial system.*

The sanctions, while only meant to hurt Russia, has also compromised the economic security of other European countries. The oil embargo against Russia drove gas prices higher, which led to the US imploring Saudi Arabia to offset this effect by flooding the market with more oil—a prospect that would hurt OPEC profit margins. Meanwhile, many of the countries reliant on Ukrainian and Russian exports are underdeveloped and are thus at great risk of severe food shortages. Eritrea imports nearly all of its wheat just from Ukraine and Russia, while other nations in Africa and Asia imports over 30% of their wheat from both countries. Ukrainian officials reported that Russia was stealing much of Ukraine's grain and sending them to Russian occupied ports for export and trade. They also reported that a vast array of farm equipment was taken from Ukrainian farms and sent to Russia. All of these acts would further exacerbate the food supply crisis and raise the risk of potential worldwide famine.

In addition to food disruption, the war in Ukraine has led to damage of critical infrastructure. The Kozarovychi Dam was struck by Russian artillery, which caused flooding near the Irpin River. Luckily, Ukraine was able to protect the Kyiv Dam because had that been destroyed, areas of Kyiv would have flooded, which would have led to the destruction of other dams along the way. Flooding in Kyiv could have made its way to the Zaphorizhzhia Power Plant and caused catastrophic damage. During the war, Russia in one of its main goals, opened the flow of water into Crimea by destroying the dam that Ukraine built on the North Crimean Canal for the sake of keeping Crimea from accessing its water flow.

There were some reports that Russian officers were killing their wounded and that Russian soldiers were killing their generals. In other reports, Russian officers have been committing suicide. Apparently some Russian soldiers were hurting themselves just to be sent home. Ukrainian intel released a phone conversation between a Russian soldier and his girlfriend in which the Russian soldier was telling her that he was planning on hurting himself so that he could be discharged. Another conversation intercepted by Ukrainian intel revealed that one Russian commander had shot himself in the leg in order to escape combat duty. Also, there have been demonstrations in Russia against the war in Ukraine, while mothers of boys drafted into the Russian army have tried to take steps to get them out of the war.

During the invasion, a number of cultural sites in Ukraine have been destroyed by Russian forces; other artifacts of high value have been relocated to Russia. Russia in fact has special ops groups designated for that main purpose. The looting of art and other historical artifacts would negatively impact Ukraine's tourism sector.

On June 29th, Ukraine and the Donetsk People's Republic carried out its largest prisoner swap of the war, each exchanging 144 soldiers previously held captive. Ukraine secured the release of 144 of its soldiers, while the DPR secured the release of 144 soldiers comprising of DPR and Russian troops. Still hundreds of Ukrainians remain unaccounted for, and are believed to be held at secret Russian detention sites. Many of the Ukrainian soldiers released during the June 29th prisoner swap were in bad condition, still suffering from shrapnel wounds and other battle injuries. 43 of those released were from the Azov regiment. Hundreds more, however, remain in captivity.

The very next day, Russian troops withdrew from Snake Island, allowing the passage of grain export. This was how Russian army spokesman Igor Konashenkov worded it, saying: "the Armed Forces of the Russian Federation finished fulfilling the assigned tasks in Snake Island and withdrew the garrison that had been operating there.......this solution will prevent Kyiv from speculating on an impending grocery crisis citing the inability to export grain due to total control of the northwestern part of the Black Sea by Russia." While Russia reported the withdrawal to be a measure of goodwill on their part, Ukraine reported that the withdrawal was a retreat on Russia's part as a result of Ukraine's constant artillery bombardment of the island. Natalia Humenyuk, a spokeswoman for the Ukrainian Military's Southern Command, said in an interview with Espresso TV "that a powerful rocket artillery assault that we have been conducting for some time, during the entire military operation, on this small enemy outpost has achieved its goal. They truly understood that they have to do the right thing, gathered their things and got out as soon as they could,"

## Chapter 13: The Prisoner Swap Deal

In the book "Anthony's Treaty," one of the main angles proposed for peace to end the Donbas War as it stood before February 24, 2022, was that Ukraine would allow water to flow into Crimea. Ukraine's blocking of the flow of water into Crimea was a major flashpoint during the Donbas conflict. Now that tensions have escalated and Russia has launched a full-scale invasion of the country, talks going forward will now require that Ukraine cede territory to Russia. This at the moment seems like the only conduit to peace. Otherwise, Ukraine's future will depend on direct western intervention which will put much of the world at risk of being impacted by a conflict where nuclear escalation would be imminent. So far, since the Russian invasion began, a number of ceasefire talks have been orchestrated. Just a few days after Russia launched their operation into Ukraine, officials from Ukraine and Russia met in Belarus to discuss setting up evacuation corridors for Ukrainian civilians, but no deal was ratified, even after meeting on three different occasions. In early March, Russia initiated a 5 ½ hour ceasefire to allow civilians to evacuate Mariupol and Volnovakha, but this was disrupted by shelling. Ukraine and Russia accused each other of violating the ceasefire. The Red Cross had gotten involved as a facilitator and admitted that attempts to establish humanitarian corridors didn't manifest. On March 7th, Russia demanded that Ukraine assert neutrality by cutting ties with NATO and canceling the intention to join the bloc, as well as recognize Crimea as part of the Russian Federation and the two breakaway regions, the Donetsk People's Republic and Luhansk People's Republic as separate from Ukraine. These demands were followed up with a ceasefire by Russian forces in Kyiv and other cities around Ukraine. Zelenskyy, throughout the war has sought to speak directly with president Putin and has stated that Ukraine will not join NATO, but will seek a security deal with other nations individually. Zelenskyy also refused to recognize Crimea as part of the Russian Federation or the breakaway regions in the Donbas as separate from Ukraine. However, Zelenskyy did say he was open to making concessions for the Russian language. On March 10th, Turkey serving as a mediator of peace between Ukraine and Russia hosted talks in Antalya. After a number of sessions, Zelenskyy agreed with many of the principles laid out by Russia as terms for peace, such as Ukraine not joining NATO. Much of the reason for Zelenskyy's acquiescence on NATO was his disappointment with NATO's response during the war and their refusal to provide Ukraine with fighter jets which, if they had been provided, would have changed the scope of the war because it would have allowed Ukraine to set up a no fly zone over the country. The talks in Turkey was the first real progress on peace terms arising between Ukraine and Russia. The plan that Russia presented had 15 points along with a direct exchange involving Russian withdrawal from western parts of Ukraine for Ukraine's decision to refrain from joining NATO. While Ukraine would disembark from plans to join NATO, they still proposed setting up a security agreement with US, Russia, UK, France, Germany, and Turkey. Despite the progress, some remained suspicious of Russia, believing that Russia was only faking as part of a military strategy of surprise. There was intelligence circulating that this could have been the case, according to French Foreign Minister Jean-Yves Le Drian. However, by March 20th, the peace talk progress continued as Russia continued to reiterate that Ukraine not join NATO and that Ukraine allow the Russian language to be protected in Ukraine. While NATO membership was a major flashpoint precipitating Russia's invasion on February 24, 2022, Russia was also adamant that Ukraine cede Crimea and the breakaway states in the Donbas region. However, Ukraine continued to present its own demands to Russia, which ultimately stalled peace talks, as Kremlin Spokesperson Dmitry Peskov put it. Russia considered Ukraine's demands to be unacceptable as Ukraine did not want to show weakness or give off the impression of being subjugated. UN Secretary-General Antonio Guterres believed that no side could win the war and that peace talks to end the fighting was imperative. Subsequently, another round of talks were set to begin in Istanbul on March 28th, and Zelenskyy was prepared to announce to Russia that Ukraine would not join NATO. Other countries like Estonia remained skeptical, citing incidents in the past when Russia would conduct peace talks, make agreements, only to later violate the terms. In April, both the Chancellor of Austria and the UN Secretary General met with Putin in Russia and noted the vast difference of perspective between that of Ukraine and that of Russia. Russia's perspective of the invasion was completely different from that of Ukraine's, and this evoked pessimism that a peace deal, at least in the short term, could be achieved. In mid-May, President Putin met with representatives from Kazakhstan, Kyrgyzstan, Armenia, Tajikistan, and Belarus to discuss measures required to deal with the possibility of NATO forces entering Ukraine and the impact that it would have on border security issues. Sweden and Finland had recently announced that they would join NATO, which led to Russia stopping all gas and oil exports to Finland and also pledging to deploy 12 Russian divisions to the Finland/Russia border. Later in May, the US attempted to get involved in the peace process through a partnership with Japan, while at the same time in provocation of China, pledging to support Taiwan militarily if China attempted to force Taiwan to join the mainland. This promise to Taiwan was incompatible with US resolve to continue to supply Ukraine with military aid, and likely further fostered mistrust of US foreign policy. After initially scoffing at Russia's attempt to get Ukraine to the negotiating table, US officials began to insinuate that Ukraine may have to end the war at the negotiating table, or in other words cede territory to Russia and the Russia-backed separatists, a prospect that President Zelenskyy of Ukraine has continued to denounce.

However, if Ukraine does not cut its losses, they will stand to lose even more territory if they continue to push back. There are examples in history where territory unjustifiably seized only led to more territory being unjustifiably seized when the native inhabitants tried to push back. Two examples of this are North America and Palestine. Many in the political world, especially on the left leaning side of the spectrum, have come to a consensus that both the Palestinians in Israel and the Native Americans in North America were unfairly pushed out of their longstanding habitat. In both cases, the indignation regarding this had no impact on the tides leaning in favor of what would be considered a fair outcome. In both cases, when these groups attempted to seize what they felt belonged to them, they only lost more territory in the process and were left having to demand that the allocation just prior to their military move be restored. But at that point it was too late. They felt emboldened by indignation and took a gamble and lost. In the case of Israel, when the military attempt by Arab forces failed and Israeli forces were able to seize more land as a result, the Arabs tried to turn back the clock and demand that the allocation of Palestine/Israel go back to the pre-1967 arrangement. But now after having seen that the Arabs were discontent when that arrangement was previously in place, Israel has no way of trusting that militant forces would stop waging war against the Jewish state if the Jewish state hypothetically agrees to a settlement going back to the 1967 allocation of Palestine. Now in the case of Ukraine, Ukrainian officials want what was on the negotiating table prior to February of 2022, when the breakaway regions in the Donbas region were still recognized by Russia as a part of Ukraine. When that situation presented itself, there was no push by Ukraine to cut one's losses and simply acquiesce to Russia's demands concerning NATO. Ukraine remained defiant and now the same perspective of wanting to go back to an earlier settlement as applied by the Arabs in their respective territory, is being applied in the case of Ukraine and will, in similar fashion, only bring more and more of Ukraine further and further under Russian control. Much like Ukraine at the moment, both the Palestinians and the Native Americans had foreign backing, which compelled them to believe that they could stop the hegemony of the stronger occupying forces. In both cases, the foreign backing had no effect. They still lost territory.

In history, the only time Ukraine was able to carve out its territory amid Russian influence was when there was regime change in Russia. This occurred when the Russian empire collapsed during the Bolshevik revolution, which allowed Ukraine to establish the central Rada and define its territorial borders. The same happened again after the Soviet Union fell, which once again allowed Ukraine to define its jurisdiction. But now, calling for regime change in the Russian Federation would have catastrophic consequences for Ukraine and would almost certainly lead to a repeat of history when Russia forcefully assumed command over all of Ukraine, much like they did during the time of the Russian empire and during the time of the Soviet Union. At the moment, while Ukraine has lost 20% of its territory, they still have much of its autonomy and can attest to successfully resisting a military force that the rest of the world was afraid of. That is a huge source of pride for Ukrainians. Another factor in Ukraine's favor at the moment is that the breakaway regions in eastern Ukraine are still not officially Russian Federation territory, although backed by

Russian military. There is still a path to concordance with the separatists that could lead to reunification in the future if the separatist are open to Kyiv making concessions on the Russian language and also taking responsibility for the tragedy of Odessa when 48 ethnic Russians were killed in a fire at the Trade Union Building. It is still possible that the DPR and LPR could in the future become open to being a federalized part of Ukraine with internal autonomy.

The best course of action would be for Ukraine to evaluate what they currently have and asses whether any moves in the future would jeopardize their own autonomy as a nation or lead to further losses. Now that Russia has already invested Russian lives for the sustaining of Russian culture/language in eastern Ukraine, there isn't much Ukraine can leverage in negotiations at the moment. They could engage the leadership of the LPR and the DPR breakaway states and maybe seek an interconnected economic relationship with them in the hopes of a future open borders scenario or scenario where the breakaway states may agree to become a federalized part of Ukraine. Any plans to Ukrainize that area of the country has to be taken off the table indefinitely.

If Ukraine continues fighting expecting to reclaim all of the former Ukrainian territories overnight, especially while assuming commitment from a historically unreliable ally in the United States, such could ultimately lead to the complete marginalization of Ukrainian people and a drastic reduction of what becomes Ukrainian territory. Continued fighting will lead to events in eastern Europe playing out much like events in Israel, when those nations that initially backed Palestinian resistance to Israeli hegemony ultimately conceded and accepted Israel's jurisdiction. Similarly as it pertains to eastern Europe, those nations which support Ukrainian resistance will ultimately demand Ukrainian capitulation when they become weary of war and bloodshed. France and the US are both now trying to push Ukraine to the negotiating table, and many of Ukraine's closest allies will follow suit. And all that will be left for Ukraine is a hatred and resentment of anything Russian. This type of hatred, much as we see harbored by Palestinians against Israel, is a hatred that cannot even be described. Just the mere mention of Israeli evokes a profound level of vitriol not normally operating on earth and among men. Ukrainians are headed in that same direction if they continue to lose ground to the Russians and witness civilian casualties, family members being obliterated by constant shelling, all of which will coincide with continued resistance. When the hate reaches such a level, any and everything associated with the enemy considered an abomination, there is nothing the enemy can do to appease, other than cease to exist. This is why the international community must develop a plan of compensation to be operated concurrent with their plan to establish accountability. It is all too often the case, that nations which maintain a powerful military apparatus are able to conduct military operations that do not follow along with international regulations on warfare. In these cases, international criminal courts can only stand by and make symbolic gestures. A fund dedicated to reparations for victims of war crimes carried out by impregnable forces will help the healing process. In this regard, there is always recourse. In this case, the victim, if he has no recourse as far as lobbying for a criminal investigation, he can apply for some sort of financial compensation.

During the conflict, Ukraine had been pressured into both ceding the breakaway regions to the separatists and ceding Crimea to Russia. Reports about Ukraine winning the war was to keep morale high, but now Ukrainian officials are admitting that the sheer size of the Russian army and the amount of equipment the Russians have is overwhelming them in the east. They subsequently demanded more artillery from the US, but some of the weapons sent are already being sold on the black market. The critical issue right now for Ukraine is orchestrating prisoner swaps and getting Ukrainians that have been deported to Russia back into Ukraine. The success of this will hinge on what Ukraine does with Viktor Medvedchuk, a close friend of Putin. Zelenskyy had offered to release Medvedchuk for Ukrainians held captive in Russia and separatist-held territories, but the Kremlin had refused the offer. Medvedchuk was a pro-Russian Ukrainian politician and a stanch ally of Putin for two decades, remaining loyal to him even after ethnic Russians voted to make Crimea a part of Russia and also after separatists seized control over Donetsk and Luhansk. According to Ukraine, both Putin and Medvedchuk have vacationed together and have close family ties. Putin is the godfather of Medvedchuk's daughter. While NATO expansion has been cited as the reason for Putin's invasion of

Ukraine, some wonder whether or not Ukraine's treatment of Medvedchuk in the years leading up to the war was another reason for Putin's antipathy towards Ukraine. Ukraine shut down Medvedchuk's media stations and also confiscated his personal assets, before charging him with treason. He served as the last link between a possible future relationship between Ukraine and Russia, and he was certainly the man that Russia wanted to be in power in Ukraine after the war would end. However, shortly after Russian forces moved into Ukraine, Medvedchuk went missing before appearing in Ukrainian custody. His capture provided Ukraine with leverage in negotiating prisoner swaps, and Zelenskyy made a proposition to Putin, saying he would *"exchange this man of yours for our boys and our girls who are now in Russian captivity"* But Russia refused the request and insisted that Medvedchuk had no special influence on Russia's politics or their geopolitical agenda.

Ukraine will have to use the prospect of recognizing both the autonomy of the breakaway states and also Crimea as part of Russia, in order to negotiate prisoner swaps and the return of Ukrainians held captive by Russia. This is a vital aspect of the war because any lack of care here can trigger a similar dynamic of which occurred between US forces and jihadists forces, where each side began abusing captives with impunity. US abuses at Guantanamo Bay have been heavily documented, and be-headings of American civilians captured by jihadists in Iraq have been aired on streaming media. This is where the international media has to conduct itself in a responsible manner that is willing to place pressure on both sides of the conflict to treat captives humanely. Both western and Russian media have to agree to stop using the word "mercenary" to describe foreign fighters. Double standards only protract tensions that impede diplomatic progress.

However when it comes to treatment of detainees, the US is in no position to lecture anyone. There is plenty of evidence that US armed forces personnel have carried out acts of torture against against individuals that had been detained and held captive in Iraq, Afghanistan, and Guantanamo Bay, Cuba. Such acts violated Article 1 of the Convention Against Torture. Many of the tortures conducted by US military personnel against detainees involved infliction of extreme pain for the sake of extracting information and carrying out punishment. In Iraq, at Abu Ghraib prison, some of the torture techniques used involved forcing detainees to maintain a stressful and painful physical position for a lengthy period of time. Many of them were stripped naked. Some were confined in darkness for long periods. Others were forced to wear women's clothing. It was also reported that detainees would in some cases be deprived of food, water and sleep. In some instances, detainees were forced to stay out in the sun in hot weather. There were physical and sexual assaults, where detainees would be forced to pose in a sexually explicit manner while being photographed. A number of detainees have died because of these aforementioned tactics. The FBI also reported that US military personnel carried out severe abuse of civilian detainees at Abu Graihib prison. These abuses, according to an FBI memo, included physical assault and strangulation, as well as mock executions. At Guantanamo Bay, similar violations of human rights occurred against detainees there—hooding, exposure to extreme weather, forced to assume stressful physical positions, sexual assaults, and being forced to strip naked. To this day, none of the perpetrators of torture have faced any accountability.

The only way to prevent a repeat of this during the Ukraine/Russia war will depend on how the international community and media remains engaged on the conflict. US tortures against detainees were carried out during a time in which the media was swayed by a pro-American narrative that would never presume that the US was capable of committing such atrocities or war crimes. Such negligence on the part of the international community and US media certainly played a role in US military personnel believing they could get away with those acts. In order to avoid a repeat where Ukraine and Russia may feel they could operate in a similar manner without scrutiny, the international community must provide ample, but fair coverage of the detainee situation in Ukraine. This is the next crucial aspect of the war that should not be overlooked. The media must get involved in urging Ukraine and Russia to do whatever it can to secure the release of captives detained by the military forces. Both sides of the conflict have already suffered too many losses to give ground over to the enemy. However, the human situation should be prioritized alongside the territorial situation. Russia should be willing to make concessions on Crimea for the sake of the release of Russian captives and volunteers held by Ukrainian forces.

While Ukraine make concessions on the breakaway regions in the Donbas in exchange for Russia and DPR/LPR forces returning Ukrainian captives to Ukraine. In the book Anthony's Treaty, it was proposed that in exchange for Ukraine allowing water into Crimea, Russia would allow Crimea to hold a referendum on which country it wants to remain a part of. This referendum would have been conducted every 10 years for 100 years. In this book "Russia's Komfort", Russia would offer to allow Crimea to hold referendums every 10 years for 100 years if Ukraine will release Russian detainees which include civilians, foreign fighters, Russian troops, as well as Mr. Medvedchuk. Ukraine, on the other hand, would offer to recognize the autonomy of the Donetsk People's Republic and the Luhansk People's Republic only on the condition that Russia release all Ukrainian captives and allow them back into Ukraine. This includes civilians, Ukrainian Azov fighters, and foreign fighters such as the two Americans currently in Russia's custody, and the British fighters/Moroccan fighter sentenced to death in the Donetsk.

This deal would be facilitated by the World Economic Forum(WEF) whom would establish a cryptocurrency fund aimed at providing reparations directly to civilian victims of the war, both Ukrainian speakers and Russian-speakers in Ukraine. The requirement for securing this funding requires that victims or immediate relatives of victims sign a document in which they agree to not pursue charges of war crimes against those parties responsible for their injuries or deaths of family members.

This fund initiated by the World Economic Forum should seek to establish the cooperation of multiple nations. The new fund would serve alongside the ICC and serve as a fill in when victims of war crimes are not able to acquire justice due to the nature and size of the perpetrator. With such an arrangement, when victims of war crimes are not able to get justice, they can receive reparations instead. And because the funding is transferred directly from the fund to the victim, the victim is ensured to receive the aid. Cryptocurrency makes the transfer all the more easier.

The World Economic Forum is an international organization that focuses on bringing together the most prominent leaders of society to discuss solutions to global issues. It was formed in Geneva Switzerland in 1971 and has been instrumental in bringing the world into a more integrated framework in which solutions to problems at the global level can be addressed. The WEF prides itself on maintaining a strong moral capacity not swayed by any political agenda, and works to gather input from all walks of life, all nationalities, for the sake of making the world a place for positive change. In recent years, however, all of the WEF's progress in making the world more interconnected has been stifled by political unrest, the Covid-19 pandemic, and the war in Ukraine, all of which is fragmenting and breaking the world apart. The residual effect of the war in Ukraine has impacted the economy at the global level, from rising energy prices and food shortages. Another issue of concern is nuclear weapons proliferation now that two nations, Libya and Ukraine, both of whom gave up their nuclear weapons in exchange for security guarantees, would end up having their territorial integrity violated by states that initially promised to respect their sovereignty on that basis. The WEF must re-integrate Russia back into the global community but only on the basis of a discussion that answers why larger powers are impervious to accountability, a precedent set by the actions of US forces in  the middle east.

Russia's invasion of Ukraine violated the UN Charter, but both Russia and Ukraine going back to 2014, as documented by human rights groups, have committed war crimes and violated international human rights laws. Both the Ukrainian forces and Russian forces have deployed military into residential areas and launched artillery strikes from those areas and thereby endangered the civilian population. Western-based human rights organizations documented this to be the case, but largely pointed out Russia as the main offender, while not having not followed up on evidence that Ukrainian forces were endangering civilian lives. Both Ukrainian and Russian forces used cluster bombs during the conflict, violating a pact signed between multiple nations banning the use of such weapons. Artillery strikes damaged soft targets such as hospitals and schools. A theater sheltering hundreds of civilians in Mariupol was struck by Russian artillery. A Russian strike damaged the Zaphorizhzhia Nuclear Power Plant. Just a month into the conflict, over 1000 civilians were killed as a result of the fighting. Another 1600 were injured. Thousands of Ukrainian civilians were deported to Russia, and during the fighting, it was alleged that Russia was summarily executing innocent civilians and raping young women. Russia has also been accused of conducting torture sessions.

Human rights organizations based in the west have not followed up on evidence implicating Ukrainian forces when it came to endangering Ukrainian civilians. It has been documented that Ukrainian forces were launching strikes from residential areas.

The ICC's Rome Statue was violated by both Russia's invasion of Ukraine and the US invasion of Iraq. According to the ICC, invasions and annexations are illegal. But Russia nor the US recognizes the ICC's jurisdiction. The court, however, as an ongoing investigation in Ukraine since 2013 regarding acts of genocide by any persons or party in the conflict. They have also been active in sending representatives to Ukraine to inspect sites of civilian casualties.

Shortly after the Russian invasion began in February, the UN Human Rights Council established a new committee to deal specifically with violations of humanitarian law in Ukraine during the war. UN Human Rights monitoring agency took note of unlawful detainment of journalists and politicians in Russian occupied areas. It was estimated that around 45 people working in the public sector had been arrested. The agency also also documented reports of human rights violations of the part of Ukrainian forces. The UN human rights monitoring has been keeping tabs on violations since 2014. Ukraine reported to have evidence of 2500 war crimes committed by Russian forces along with the names of many of the suspects. During the war, one person from the Russian forces as brought to trial to face charges of killing an unarmed civilian.

Russia, prior to the invasion, considered Ukraine's blocking of water flow into Crimea a form of genocide. In lieu of that, Russia justified the invasion on that basis. However, Ukraine contested this by going to the International Court of Justice(ICJ) which forbids false allegation of genocide as a pretext for invasion. This is part of the Genocide Convention of 1948, an accordance which both Ukraine and Russia have signed onto. The ICJ ruled in March that Russia was in violation and ordered them to disengage from Ukraine.

The war in Ukraine has exposed double standards within the international community. If these double standards are not addressed within an international forum, the world will continue to become more polarized. Also, the international human rights community needs to define itself in terms of where it stands on justice and peace because in many cases the two are not compatible. The aims of many separatists groups and nations are not peaceful in any way shape or form because their demands to "right" a previous "wrong" require the loss of civilian lives. For this reason the entities like the World Economic Forum, NGOs, and the United Nations have to asses what its main goals are. If it is justice, then they should prepare to accept the reality that innocent lives will be lost in that process. If it is peace, then they must accept the reality that justice will be lost in the process. Should the international community choose the latter, then all war crimes investigations against both Ukraine and Russia's high ranking government officials, thanks in part to US impunity in the middle east, have to be dropped once a ceasefire is established. Then, every effort has to be taken to compensate the victims of the conflict in some other manner. Another important step is making sure every effort is being taken to secure the release of everyone held captive as a result of the war. This includes fighters, civilians and volunteers. Following this, a new convention needs to be established when it comes to the laws of war, one that will have something else in place when accountability cannot be established.

# Bibliography


"Ukraine: Russian Forces' Trail of Death in Bucha
Preserving Evidence Critical for War Crimes Prosecutions"
https://www.hrw.org/news/2022/04/21/ukraine-russian-forces-
trail-death-bucha
(This source was used in Chapter 3 to explain how Human Rights
Watch documented the Bucha Massacre)

Wikipedia contributors. (2022, June 19). 2014 Odessa clashes. In
Wikipedia, The Free Encyclopedia. Retrieved 16:11, June 21, 2022,
from https://en.wikipedia.org/w/index.php?
title=2014_Odessa_clashes&oldid=1093953691
(This source was used to explain the Odessa fire in the
Introduction section)

Ukrainian unrest spreads as dozens killed in Odessa
https://www.france24.com/en/20140502-dozens-killed-building-
fire-ukraine-odessa-clashes-pro-russia-activists
(This source was used to explain the Odessa fire)

https://carnegieeurope.eu/2018/09/12/how-eastern-ukraine-is-
adapting-and-surviving-case-of-kharkiv-pub-77216
(This source was used to explain the situation in Kharkiv prior to
Feb 24, 2022)

Wikipedia contributors. (2022, April 20). Criticism of Human
Rights Watch. In Wikipedia, The Free Encyclopedia. Retrieved
16:18, June 21, 2022, from https://en.wikipedia.org/w/index.php?
title=Criticism_of_Human_Rights_Watch&oldid=1083779764
(This source was used on pg 33 to explain criticism of HRW)

SUMMARY KILLINGS DURING THE CONFLICT IN EASTERN
UKRAINE by Amnesty International
https://www.amnesty.eu/wp-content/uploads/2018/10/Ukraine.p

<u>df</u>   (this source was used on pages 44 and 45 to explain Ukraine's war crimes in the Donbas region before Russian invasion)

"HE'S NOT COMING BACK" WAR CRIMES IN NORTHWEST AREAS OF KYIV OBLAST First published in 2022 by Amnesty International Ltd Peter Benenson House, 1 Easton Street, London WC1X 0DW, UK(this report was used a source on pg 48 and in other areas of the book)

100,000 Iraqi civilians dead, says study - Article by Sarah Boseley <u>https://www.theguardian.com/world/2004/oct/29/iraq.sarahbos</u> <u>eley</u>   (this source was used on page 73)

Iraq's bloodiest battle will be a video game By Alaa Elassar, CNN <u>https://lite.cnn.com/en/article/h_be54549e672188884b44322316</u> <u>d0777a</u> (this source was used on page 77 to explain war crimes by US soldiers)

Wikipedia contributors. (2022, June 13). Mahmudiyah rape and killings. In Wikipedia, The Free Encyclopedia. Retrieved 16:54, June 21, 2022, from <u>https://en.wikipedia.org/w/index.php?</u> <u>title=Mahmudiyah_rape_and_killings&oldid=1092983734</u> (pages 82 and 83 uses this source to explain rapes carried out by US soldiers)

The Haditha shootings: What the witnesses saw by Josh White <u>https://www.seattletimes.com/nation-world/the-haditha-</u> <u>shootings-what-the-witnesses-saw/</u> (this source is used on pg 79 and 80 to explain the Haditha Massacre)

<u>https://carnegieeurope.eu/2018/09/12/how-eastern-ukraine-is-</u> <u>adapting-and-surviving-case-of-kharkiv-pub-77216</u>

LIBYA THE FORGOTTEN VICTIMS OF NATO STRIKES Amnesty International 2012 <u>https://www.amnesty.org/en/wp-content/uploads/2021/07/mde1</u> <u>90032012en.pdf</u> (uses this source on pages 8 and 9 to explain NATO war crimes)

<u>https://www.hrw.org/sites/default/files/reports/natbm002.pdf</u> CIVILIAN DEATHS IN THE NATO AIR CAMPAIGN

Who is Viktor Medvedchuk and why does his arrest matter to the Kremlin?
https://www.theguardian.com/world/2022/apr/13/viktor-medvedchuk-arrest-matter-to-kremlin (pages 126 – 129 uses this source to explain capture of Medvedchuk)

Putin says Russia to use Middle East volunteer fighters
https://www.reuters.com/world/europe/putin-says-volunteers-welcome-help-fight-against-ukrainian-forces-2022-03-11/ (pg 106 uses this source to explain how Reuters calls Russian volunteers mercenaries)

American fighters who surrendered in Donbass speak to RT
https://www.rt.com/news/557340-us-fighters-captured-ukraine/ (uses this source to document on pg 107 how Russian fighters captured American volunteers in Ukraine)

American Fighters, Ukraine, and the Neutrality Act: The Law and the Urgent Need for Clarity by Dakota Rudesill
https://www.justsecurity.org/80612/american-fighters-ukraine-and-the-neutrality-act-the-law-and-the-urgent-need-for-clarity/ (used this source to explain the Neutrality Act on pg 108)

Ukraine war: Britons Aiden Aslin and Shaun Pinner sentenced to death https://www.bbc.com/news/uk-61745556 (pg 106 uses this source)

Wikipedia contributors. (2022, June 21). 2022 Russian invasion of Ukraine. In Wikipedia, The Free Encyclopedia. Retrieved 16:44, June 21, 2022, from https://en.wikipedia.org/w/index.php?title=2022_Russian_invasion_of_Ukraine&oldid=1094244748 (This source was used to document the Russian war in Ukraine and other events)

Wikipedia contributors. (2022, June 21). Siege of Mariupol. In Wikipedia, The Free Encyclopedia. Retrieved 16:45, June 21, 2022, from https://en.wikipedia.org/w/index.php?title=Siege_of_Mariupol&oldid=1094257054

(this source was used in chapter 6 to explain the siege of Mariupol)

Wikipedia contributors. (2022, June 21). Battle of Sievierodonetsk (2022). In Wikipedia, The Free Encyclopedia. Retrieved 16:47, June 21, 2022, from https://en.wikipedia.org/w/index.php?title=Battle_of_Sievierodonetsk_(2022)&oldid=1094229854
(Chapter 11 uses this source to explain battle of Sievierodonetsk)


Wikipedia contributors. (2022, June 20). Bucha massacre. In Wikipedia, The Free Encyclopedia. Retrieved 16:48, June 21, 2022, from https://en.wikipedia.org/w/index.php?title=Bucha_massacre&oldid=1094073072
(Chapter 2 uses this source to summarize the Bucha massacre)

Wikipedia contributors. (2022, June 11). Nisour Square massacre. In Wikipedia, The Free Encyclopedia. Retrieved 16:50, June 21, 2022, from https://en.wikipedia.org/w/index.php?title=Nisour_Square_massacre&oldid=1092571806
(Pages 81 and 82 uses this source to explain the Blackwater massacre)

TORTURE BY THE UNITED STATES The Status of Compliance by the U.S. Government with the International Convention Against Torture and Other Cruel, Inhuman and Degrading Treatment or Punishment Submitted to the United Nation's Committee Against Torture in conjunction with the expected filing by the U.S. Government in January, 2005 of their report on compliance with CAT standards by The World Organization for Human Rights USA Morton Sklar, Executive Director and
 Jenny-Brooke Condon, Litigation Director
January 2005
https://www2.ohchr.org/english/bodies/hrc/docs/ngos/wohr.pdf
(pages 127 and 128 uses this source to describe US tortures of detainees)

NATO/FEDERAL REPUBLIC OF YUGOSLAVIA
"COLLATERAL DAMAGE" OR UNLAWFUL KILLINGS?
Violations of the Laws of War by NATO during Operation Allied Force (pg 9 uses this source)

## A



## B

www.ingramcontent.com/pod-product-compliance
Lightning Source LLC
Chambersburg PA
CBHW051306250726
48656CB00004B/1506